AMERICAN

DIRECTORY OF

JOB AND

LABOR MARKET

INFORMATION

First Edition

Career Communications, Inc.

2   3   4   5   6   7   8   9   10

The publisher has made every reasonable attempt to obtain and verify the information contained herein. However, the publisher does not warrant that the information is complete and accurate; nor does the publisher guarantee job availability or employment; and does not assume any loss or damage as a result of errors or omissions which may occur.

ISBN 1-881587-01-0

A MESSAGE FROM THE PUBLISHER

Dear Reader,

Our government represents the largest source of job and career information in the United States. Yet very few people know how to tap into this vast informational resource. Most of us are simply unaware that the data exists or are intimidated by the time and costs required to track down this vital career information.

That's why we created the **American Directory of Job and Labor Market Information.** The directory is specifically designed to be an easy-to-read, one-stop source to pinpoint federal, state, and city government employment resources nationwide. Your taxes pay for these programs and resources. Why not take full advantage of them in support of your job search campaign or to enhance your career library?

We thank you for selecting the **American Directory of Job and Labor Market Information** and sincerely hope the directory will help you connect with information and resources to make your future plans a success.

Best wishes,

Steven A. Wood

Steven A. Wood
Publisher

Career Communications, Inc. • P. O. Box 169 • Harleysville, PA 19438 • Telephone (215) 256-3130 • Fax (215) 256-3136

DISCLAIMER

This directory was researched and compiled by the editorial staff at Career Communications, Inc. While we have taken reasonable measures to ensure the validity of the listings, we cannot guarantee total accuracy. Mistakes and omissions may be typographical, the result of changes that have taken place during the shelf life of the directory, respondent errors, or our own mistakes. We welcome your comments should you identify any errors or changes.

ATTENTION: SCHOOLS, ORGANIZATIONS, CORPORATIONS

This book is available at quantity discounts for bulk purchases
for educational, business or sales promotional use.
Please call 1-800-346-1848 or write:
Career Communications, Inc., 298 Main Street,
P. O. Box 169, Harleysville, PA 19438.

This publication is dedicated to the scores of government officials whose patience, courtesy and cooperation have made this directory possible.

Career Communications, Inc. • P. O. Box 169 • Harleysville, PA 19438 • Telephone (215) 256-3130 • Fax (215) 256-3136

STATE PUBLICATIONS

The following section features an alphabetical listing of state agencies that provide job and labor market publications. Most of the publications are free or low-cost items. Please contact each state agency for information and details prior to ordering.

ALABAMA

Department: Alabama Department of Industrial Relations

Publications: *The Alabama "Job Finder," Alabama Career Exploration Guide, Alabama Labor Market News, Alabama Occupational Employment, Alabama Occupational Trends for 2000.*

Address: Research & Statistics Division, 649 Monroe St., Room 422, Montgomery, AL 36103-5690

Telephone: (205) 242-8855

ALASKA

Department: Alaska Department of Labor Research & Statistics Section

Publications: *Alaska Career Guide, Alaska Directory of Licensed Occupations, Alaska Economic Trends, Alaska Occupational Supply & Demand, Alaska Industry–Occupation Outlook to 1995.*

Address: P.O. Box 25501, Juneau, AK 99802-5501

Telephone: (907) 465-4500

ARIZONA

Department: Arizona Department of Economic Security Research Administration

Publications: *Applying for Government Jobs, Helpful Hints for Job Seekers, The Job Interview, Job Seekers Guide, Employment Interview Guide, Summer Jobs for Students, Job Leads – Where to Look.*

Address: Labor Market Information, Site Code 733A, P.O. Box 6123, Phoenix, AZ 85005-6123

Telephone: (602) 542-3871

ARKANSAS

Department: Arkansas Employment Security Division, LMI Section

Publications: *Job Hunters Guide to Arkansas, Industrial and Occupational Trends 1986-2000, Arkansas Career Watch.*

Address: P.O. Box 2981, Little Rock, AR 72203-2981

Telephone: (501) 682-1543

CALIFORNIA

Department: California Employment Development Department Employment Data and Research Division

Publications: *California Labor Market Information Publication Directory, Calif. Labor Market Forecast, Calif. Occupational Guides, Calif. Labor Market Bulletin, Career Decision Making Using Labor Market Information, Projections of Employment by Industry and Occupation.*

Address: P.O. Box 942880, MIC57, Sacramento, CA 94280

Telephone: (916) 427-4675

COLORADO

Department: Colorado Department of Labor & Employment – Labor Market Information

Publications: *Colorado Labor Market Information Directory, Doing Your Best in the Employment Interview, Pocket Resume, Job Service of Colorado, Merchandising Your Job Talents, Facts About Living in Colorado.*

Address: 251 East 12th Avenue, Denver, CO 80203

Telephone: (303) 937-4926

CONNECTICUT

Department: Connecticut Labor Department – Employment Security Division, Office of Research & Information

Publications: *"Jobs–Jobs–Jobs," Labor Market Review, Occupations in Demand, Adult Education & Training Directory, Private Occupational Schools Directory.*

Address: 200 Folly Brook Blvd., Wethersfield, CT 06109

Telephone: (203) 566-2120

DELAWARE

Department: Delaware Department of Labor, Office of Occupational & Labor Information

Publications: *Delaware Jobs 2005 – An Overview, Delaware Monthly Labor Report, Delaware Labor Market Information Directory, Delaware Digest.*

Address: P.O. Box 9029, Newark, DE 19714-9029

Telephone: (302) 368-6960

DISTRICT OF COLUMBIA

Department: Department of Employment Services

Publications: *Top 200 Major Employers in the District of Columbia.*

Address: 500 C Street NW, Room 201, Washington, DC 20001

Telephone: (202) 639-1642

FLORIDA

Department:	Florida Dept. of Labor & Employment Security Bureau of Labor Market Information
Publications:	*Florida Labor Market Information Directory of Resources, Catalog of Regulated Occupations, Florida Occupational Employment Reports and Directory of Occupations, Vocational Education Programs.*
Address:	2012 Capital Circle SE, Suite 200, Hartman Building, Tallahassee, FL 32399-2151
Telephone:	(904) 488-1048

GEORGIA

Department:	Georgia Dept. of Labor, Labor Information Systems
Publications:	*Georgia Directory of Labor Market Information, Georgia Labor Market Trends.*
Address:	Sussex Place, 148 International Blvd. NE, Atlanta, GA 30303-1751
Telephone:	(404) 656-3177

HAWAII

Department:	Hawaii Department of Labor & Industry Relations Employment Security
Publications:	*How to Find a Job with Job Search Information, Demand Occupations in Hawaii, Licensed Occupations in Hawaii, Labor Area News.*
Address:	P.O. Box 3680, Honolulu, HI 96811
Telephone:	(808) 586-9028

IDAHO

Department: Idaho Department of Employment Research & Analysis Bureau

Publications: *Idaho Labor Market Information Index, Idaho Employment Monthly Newsletter, Area Employment Newsletters.*

Address: 317 Main Street, Boise, ID 83757-0670

Telephone: (208) 334-6168

ILLINOIS

Department: Illinois Department of Employment Security

Publications: *Illinois Labor Market Review, Illinois at Work, Affirmative Action Information, Illinois Occupational Projections, Where Workers Work, Illinois Labor Market Information Directory.*

Address: Economic Information and Analysis, 401 South State Street, Chicago, IL 60605

Telephone: (312) 793-2316

INDIANA

Department: Indiana Department of Employment and Training Services, Labor Market Information

Publications: *Indiana Labor Market Letter, Job Service Openings & Starting Wages Report, Indiana's Occupational Employment Projections 1984–1995.*

Address: 10 North Senate Avenue, Indianapolis, IN 46204

Telephone: (317) 232-8480

IOWA

Department:	Iowa Department of Employment Services, Labor Market Information
Publications:	*Iowa Labor Market Information Directory, Iowa Employment Review, Iowa Licensed Occupations, Iowa Wage Survey.*
Address:	1000 East Grand, Des Moines, IA 50319
Telephone:	(515) 281-3439

KANSAS

Department:	Kansas Department of Human Resources, Labor Market Information Services
Publications:	*Labor Market Information Publications Directory, Kansas Monthly Employment Review, Labor Market Summary.*
Address:	401 S.W. Topeka Blvd., Topeka, KS 66603-3182
Telephone:	(913) 296-5058

KENTUCKY

Department:	Kentucky Department for Employment Services, Labor Market Research & Analysis
Publications:	*100 Jobs for a New Century, Occupational Outlook, Labor Force Estimates, Occupational Profiles, Kentucky Labor Market Information Newsletter, Kentucky Labor Market Information Directory.*
Address:	275 East Main Street, Frankfort, KY 40621
Telephone:	(502) 564-7976

LOUISIANA

Department:	Louisiana Department of Employment & Training, Research and Statistics Unit
Publications:	*Louisiana Job Seekers Guide, Louisiana State Labor Market Information, Employment and Wages.*
Address:	P.O. Box 94094, Baton Rouge, LA 70804-9094
Telephone:	(504) 342-3141

MAINE

Department:	Maine Department of Labor, Division of Economic Analysis & Research
Publications:	*Labor Market Information Directory, Directory of Occupational Licensing, Careers in the Maine Woods, Trends in the Maine Labor Market, Labor Market Digest, Labor Market Information Services, The Maine Connection, Where Do I Begin?: Job Hunting in Maine.*
Address:	Attention: Publications Unit Manager, P.O. Box 309, Augusta, ME 04332-0309
Telephone:	(207) 289-2271

MARYLAND

Department:	Maryland Department of Economic and Employment Development
Publications:	*Maryland 1986-2000: Industry and Occupational Employment Projections, Labor Market in Review, Maryland Industrial Profile, Maryland High Technology 1990 Update.*
Address:	Office of Labor Market Analysis and Information, 1100 North Eutaw St., Baltimore, MD 21201
Telephone:	(410) 333-5000

MASSACHUSETTS

Department: MOICE Department of Employment & Training

Publications: *Directory of Licensed Occupations in Massachusetts, High Technology Careers: A Second Look.*

Address: 19 Staniford Street, 2nd Floor, Boston, MA 02114

Telephone: (617) 727-6718

MICHIGAN

Department: Michigan Employment Security Commission, Bureau of Research and Statistics

Publications: *Labor Market Review, Michigan Occupation/Industry Outlook 1995, Michigan Career Outlook 2000.*

Address: 7310 Woodward Avenue, Detroit, MI 48202

Telephone: (313) 876-5439

MINNESOTA

Department: Minnesota Department of Jobs & Training Research Office, Research & Statistical Services

Publications: *Minnesota Careers, Minnesota Employment, Minnesota Labor Market Review.*

Address: 390 North Robert Street, St. Paul, MN 55101

Telephone: (612) 296-6545

MISSISSIPPI

Department:	Mississippi Employment Security Commission, Labor Market Information Department
Publications:	*Guide to Labor Market Information, Labor Market Trends, Mississippi Labor Market.*
Address:	P.O. Box 1699, Jackson, MS 39215-1699
Telephone:	(601) 961-7452

MISSOURI

Department:	Missouri Division of Employment Security, Research & Analysis
Publications:	*Missouri Area Labor Trends, Industry Employment Data, Labor Force Data, Area Wage Surveys, Labor Market Information for Affirmative Action Programs, Mass Layoff Statistics.*
Address:	P.O. Box 59, Jefferson City, MO 65104-0059
Telephone:	(314) 751-3591

MONTANA

Department:	Montana Department of Labor and Industry Research and Analysis Bureau
Publications:	*Licensed Occupations in Montana, Montana's Growing and Declining Occupations 1986-1995, Montana Employment and Labor Force Trends.*
Address:	P.O. Box 1728, 1327 Lockey, Helena, MT 59624
Telephone:	(406) 444-2430

NEBRASKA

Department:	Nebraska Department of Labor, Labor Market Information
Publications:	*Careers in Nebraska, Finding a Job in the Want Ads, Licensed and Certified Occupations in Nebraska, Your Job... Will You Keep It... or Lose It?*
Address:	P.O. Box 94600, Lincoln, NE 68509
Telephone:	(402) 475-8451

NEVADA

Department:	Nevada Employment Security Department, Employment Security Research Section
Publications:	*Nevada Directory of Labor Market Information Employment Guide, Job Finding Techniques, Employment Guide to Nevada State Government.*
Address:	500 East Third Street, Carson City, NV 89713
Telephone:	(702) 687-4550

NEW HAMPSHIRE

Department:	New Hampshire Employment Security, Economic & Labor Market Information Bureau
Publications:	*Directory of New Hampshire Labor Market Information, New Hampshire Employment Projections by Industry and Occupation, Employment and Wages by County.*
Address:	32 South Main Street, Concord, NH 03301-4857
Telephone:	(603) 228-4123

NEW JERSEY

Department: New Jersey Department of Labor,
Office of Research and Planning

Publications: *New Jersey Publications and Resource Directory,
Licensed Occupations in New Jersey, Regional Labor
Market Review.*

Address: Publications, Room 203, CN056, Trenton, NJ 08625

Telephone: (609) 292-7567

NEW MEXICO

Department: New Mexico Department of Labor,
Bureau of Economic Research and Analysis

Publications: *New Mexico Labor Market Information Directory, New
Mexico Occupational Outlook to 2000, Area Job Market
Flyers, New Mexico Job Hunter's Guide, New Mexico
Occupational Profiles.*

Address: P.O. Box 1928, Albuquerque, NM 87103

Telephone: (505) 841-8645

NEW YORK

Department: New York State Department of Labor,
Bureau of Labor Market Information

Publications: *New York Employment Review, A Guide to Career
Opportunities in New York State Government, Directory
of Labor Unions and Employee Organizations in New
York State, The Industry Finder: Relating Occupations
& Industries, Suggestions for Career Exploration and
Job Seeking.*

Address: Publications Unit, NY State Dept. of Labor, Room
401, Building 12, State Campus, Albany, NY 12240

Telephone: (518) 457-1130

NORTH CAROLINA

Department:	Employment Security Commision of North Carolina, Labor Market Information Division
Publications:	*North Carolina Labor Market Information Directory, Employment Trends, North Carolina Occupational Guides, Getting Started: North Carolina Jobs & Careers, Occupations Which Require Licensing in North Carolina.*
Address:	P.O. Box 25903, Raleigh, NC 27611-5903
Telephone:	(919) 733-2936

NORTH DAKOTA

Department:	North Dakota Job Service
Publications:	*North Dakota Career Outlook, Job Bank Index, North Dakota Employment and Earnings, North Dakota Directory of Labor Market and Occupational Information.*
Address:	Labor Market Information, P.O. Box 1537, Bismarck, ND 58502-1537
Telephone:	(701) 224-2868

OHIO

Department:	Ohio Bureau of Employment Services, Labor Market Information Division
Publications:	*Labor Market Review, Occupational Employment Statistics, Ohio Occupational Almanac.*
Address:	145 S. Front St., P.O. Box 1618, Columbus, OH 43216
Telephone:	(614) 466-2689

OKLAHOMA

Department: Oklahoma State Occupational Information
Coordinating Committee

Publications: *Licensed Occupations in Oklahoma, Work Force
Oklahoma, Oklahoma Career Choices.*

Address: 1500 West Seventh Ave.,
Stillwater, OK 74074-4364

Telephone: (405) 743-5197

OREGON

Department: Oregon Department of Human Resources,
Employment Division

Publications: *Oregon Labor Market Information Directory, Oregon
Wage Information, Oregon Labor Trends, Directory of
Licensed Occupations, Oregon Careers.*

Address: Attention: Research & Statistics, Room 207,
875 Union Street NE, Salem, OR 97311

Telephone: (503) 378-6400

PENNSYLVANIA

Department: Pennsylvania Department of Labor and Industry

Publications: *Merchandising Your Job Talents, How to Get the Right
Job, The Incredible Jobs Machine (Alex), My Personal
Job Search Plan, Need a Job? Get Help from Job Service.*

Address: Labor and Industry Building, Harrisburg, PA 17120

Telephone: (717) 787-7530

RHODE ISLAND

Department: Rhode Island Department of Employment and Training, Labor Market Information Unit

Publications: *Directory of Labor Market Information, Rhode Island Employment Bulletin, Rhode Island Occupational Projections to 2000, Consumers Guide to Rhode Island State Vocational Rehabilitation Services.*

Address: 101 Friendship Street, Providence, RI 02903

Telephone: (401) 277-3730

SOUTH CAROLINA

Department: South Carolina Employment Security Commission, Labor Market Information Division

Publications: *South Carolina Labor Market Information Guide, Job Search Assistance Guide, Working Women of Today and Tomorrow, Employment Trends.*

Address: P.O. Box 995, Columbia, SC 29202

Telephone: (803) 737-2660

SOUTH DAKOTA

Department: South Dakota Department of Labor, Labor Market Information Center

Publications: *South Dakota Directory of Labor Market Information, South Dakota Labor Bulletin, South Dakota Occupational Outlook Handbook, South Dakota Occupational Wage Information.*

Address: P.O. Box 4730, Aberdeen, SD 57402-4730

Telephone: (605) 622-2314

TENNESSEE

Department:	Tennessee Department of Employment Security, LMI Unit, Research & Statistics
Publications:	*Tennessee Labor Market Information Directory, Licensed Occupations in Tennessee, Women in the Labor Force, Occupations in Demand at Tennessee Department of Employment Security.*
Address:	500 James Robertson Parkway, Volunteer Plaza, 11th Floor, Nashville, TN 37245-1040
Telephone:	(615) 741-1729

TEXAS

Department:	Texas Employment Commission, Economic Research & Analysis
Publications:	*Texas Occupational Wages, Industry and Occupational Projections to the Year 2000, Texas Labor Market Review.*
Address:	15th & Congress Avenues, Room 208T, Austin, TX 78778
Telephone:	(512) 463-2616

UTAH

Department:	Utah Department of Employment Security, Attention: Labor Market Information Services, Support Services Unit
Publications:	*Helpful Hints for Job Seekers, Licensed Occupations in Utah, Utah's Career Guide, Utah Job Outlook for Occupations, 1992-1997.*
Address:	140 East 300 South, P.O. Box 11249, Salt Lake City, UT 84147
Telephone:	(801) 536-7811

VERMONT

Department: Vermont Department of Employment & Training, Policy and Information Division

Publications: *Directory of Labor Market, Career, and Occupational Information, Licensed Occupations in Vermont, The Vermont Labor Market, Vermont Occupational Projections to 2000, How to Write a Winning Resume, Job Hunt Workbook, Merchandising Your Job Talents.*

Address: P.O. Box 488, 5 Green Mountain Drive, Montpelier, VT 05601-0488

Telephone: (802) 828-4202

VIRGINIA

Department: Commonwealth of Virginia, Virginia Employment Commission

Publications: *Job Service Registration Kit, Listings of State Job Opportunities, State Job Applications, Directory of State Agency Personnel Offices.*

Address: 703 East Main Street, P.O. Box 1358, Richmond, VA 23211

Telephone: (804) 371-8050

WASHINGTON

Department: Washington State Employment Security Department, LMEA Branch

Publications: *User's Guide to Labor Market Information, Washington Labor Market, Occupational Projections, Labor Force and Employment in Washington State.*

Address: 212 Maple Park, MS: KG-11, Olympia, WA 98504-5311

Telephone: (206) 438-4800

WEST VIRGINIA

Department: State of West Virginia, Bureau of Employment Programs, Labor & Economic Research

Publications: *State of West Virginia Directory of Publications; West Virginia Occupational Projections, Licensed Occupations in West Virginia.*

Address: 112 California Avenue, Charleston, WV 25305-0112

Telephone: (304) 558-2660

WISCONSIN

Department: Wisconsin Department of Industry, Labor and Human Relations, Employment & Training Library

Publications: *Wisconsin Labor Market Information, A Reference Guide and Directory of Wisconsin Publications, Career Connections, Employment Review, Wisconsin Works, Career Opportunities Guide.*

Address: 201 East Washington Avenue, P.O. Box 7944, Madison, WI 53707-7944

Telephone: (608) 267-9613

WYOMING

Department: Wyoming Occupational Coordinating Council

Publications: *Industry and Occupational Projections for the State of Wyoming: 1990 through 1996, The Wyoming Directory of Licensed Occupations, Wyoming Career Explorer.*

Address: 246 South Center, P.O. Box 2760, Casper, WY 82602

Telephone: (307) 265-7017

1

STATE PERSONNEL OFFICES

The following section features an alphabetical listing of state personnel and employment departments found throughout the United States. Recorded jobline telephone numbers are listed where available.

ALABAMA

Department: State Personnel Department

Address: State of Alabama
402 State Administration Building
64 N. Union Street
Montgomery, AL 36130

Telephone: (205) 242-3389   **Jobline:** (205) 242-3672

ALASKA

Department: Division of Personnel

Address: State of Alaska
P. O. Box 110201
Juneau, AK 99811-0201

Telephone: (907) 465-4430

ARIZONA

Department: Personnel Division

Address: State of Arizona
1831 W. Jefferson
Phoenix, AZ 85007

Telephone: (602) 542-5216   **Jobline:** (602) 542-4966

ARKANSAS

Department: Office of Personnel Management

Address: State of Arkansas
1509 W. 7th
Little Rock, AR 72203

Telephone: (501) 682-1823   **Jobline:** (501) 682-JOBS

CALIFORNIA

Department: California Personnel Board

Address: State of California
801 Capitol Mall
Sacramento, CA 94244-2010

Telephone: (916) 653-1705

COLORADO

Department: Department of Personnel

Address: State of Colorado
1313 Sherman Street
Denver, CO 80203

Telephone: (303) 866-2321

CONNECTICUT

Department: Personnel & Labor Relations

Address: State of Connecticut
165 Capitol Avenue
Hartford, CT 06106

Telephone: (203) 566-8261

DELAWARE

Department: State Personnel Office

Address: State of Delaware
Townsend Building, P.O. Box 1401
Dover, DE 19903

Telephone: (302) 739-5458

FLORIDA

Department: Dept. of Management Services

Address: State of Florida
235 Carlton Building
Tallahassee, FL 32399-1550

Telephone: (904) 487-1749   **Jobline: (904) 487-2851**

GEORGIA

Department: Personnel Administration Office

Address: State of Georgia
200 Piedmont Ave., Room 504, West Tower
Atlanta, GA 30334

Telephone:
(404) 656-2705

HAWAII

Department: Department of Recruitment & Examination

Address: State of Hawaii
830 Punchbowl St., 4th Floor
Honolulu, HI 96813

Telephone: (808) 587-0977

IDAHO

Department: Department of Personnel

Address: State of Idaho
700 W. State St.
Boise, ID 83720

Telephone: (208) 334-3345   **Jobline: (208) 334-2568**

ILLINOIS

Department: Central Management Services

Address: State of Illinois
William D. Stratton Building
401 S. Spring, Room 500
Springfield, IL 62706

Telephone: (217) 782-7110

INDIANA

Department: Department of Personnel

Address: State of Indiana
402 W. Washington St., R-W161
Indianapolis, IN 46204

Telephone: (317) 232-3059

IOWA

Department: Department of Personnel

Address: State of Iowa
Grimes State Office Building
E. 14th & Grand
Des Moines, IA 50319

Telephone: (515) 281-3351   **Jobline:** (515) 281-5820

KANSAS

Department: Division of Personnel Services

Address: State of Kansas
Landon State Office Building
9th & Jackson St., Room 951-S
Topeka, KS 66612

Telephone: (913) 296-4278   **Jobline:** (913) 296-2208

KENTUCKY

Department: Department of Personnel

Address: State of Kentucky
Division of Application Counseling
Capitol Annex, Room 249
Frankfort, KY 40601

Telephone: (502) 564-4460

LOUISIANA

Department: Department of Civil Service

Address: State of Louisiana
1201 Capitol Station, Box 94111
Baton Rouge, LA 70804-9111

Telephone: (504) 342-8536

MAINE

Department: Bureau of Human Resources

Address: State of Maine
State Office Building, Station #4
Augusta, ME 04333

Telephone: (207) 289-3761

MARYLAND

Department: Department of Personnel Administration

Address: State of Maryland
301 W. Preston Street, Room 609
Baltimore, MD 21201

Telephone: (410) 225-4715

MASSACHUSETTS

Department: Dept. of Employment & Training

Address: State of Massachusetts
Claims Department
Charles Hurley Bldg., 19 Staniford St.
Boston, MA 02114

Telephone: (617) 727-6718

MICHIGAN

Department: Department of Civil Service

Address: State of Michigan
Capitol Commons Center
400 S. Pine., P.O. Box 30002
Lansing, MI 48909

Telephone: (517) 373-3030

MINNESOTA

Department: Department of Employee Relations

Address: State of Minnesota
Centennial Building, Suite 200
658 Cedar St.
St. Paul, MN 55155

Telephone: (612) 297-1184

MISSISSIPPI

Department: State Personnel Board

Address: State of Mississippi
301 North Lamar
Jackson, MS 39201

Telephone: (601) 359-1406

MISSOURI

Department: Division of Personnel

Address: State of Missouri
P.O. Box 388
Jefferson City, MO 65102

Telephone: (314) 751-4162

MONTANA

Department: Department of Administation

Address: Personnel Office (Job Services Packet)
State of Montana
176 Mitchell Building
Helena, MT 59620

Telephone: (406) 444-4644

NEBRASKA

Department: Department of Personnel

Address: State of Nebraska
301 Centennial Mall South
P.O. Box 94905
Lincoln, NE 68509-4905

Telephone: (402) 471-2075

NEVADA

Department: Department of Personnel

Address: State of Nevada
209 E. Musser St.
Carson City, NV 89710

Telephone: (702) 687-4050   **Jobline:** (702) 687-4160

NEW HAMPSHIRE

Department: Division of Personnel

Address: State of New Hampshire
State House Annex, School Street
Concord, NH 03301

Telephone: (603) 271-3261

NEW JERSEY

Department: Department of Personnel

Address: State of New Jersey
Station Plaza 3, CN 311
Trenton, NJ 08625

Telephone: (609) 984-7812

NEW MEXICO

Department: State Personnel Office

Address: State of New Mexico
810 W. San Mateo, P.O. Box 26127
Sante Fe, NM 87502-0127

Telephone: (505) 827-8190

NEW YORK

Department: Department of Civil Services

Address: State of New York
Building 1
State Campus Building
Albany, NY 12239

Telephone: (518) 457-6216

NORTH CAROLINA

Department: Office of State Personnel

Address: State of North Carolina
116 W. Jones Street
Raleigh, NC 27603

Telephone: (919) 733-7922

NORTH DAKOTA

Department: Central Personnel Division

Address: State of North Dakota
State Capitol, 600 E. Boulevard Ave.
Bismarck, ND 58505-0120

Telephone: (701) 224-3290

OHIO

Department: Department of Administration Services

Address: State of Ohio
30 E. Broad Street, B-1 Level
Columbus, OH 43266

Telephone: (614) 466-4026

OKLAHOMA

Department: Office of Personnel Management

Address: State of Oklahoma
2101 N. Lincoln Blvd.
Oklahoma City, OK 73105

Telephone: (405) 521-2171

OREGON

Department: Personnel & Labor Relations Division

Address: State of Oregon
155 Cottage St. NE
Salem, OR 97310

Telephone: (503) 378-2827   **Jobline:** (503) 373-1199

PENNSYLVANIA

Department: Division of State Employment

Address: State of Pennsylvania
110 Finance Building
Harrisburg, PA 17120

Telephone: (717) 787-5703

RHODE ISLAND

Department: Office of Personnel Administration

Address: State of Rhode Island
One Capitol Hill
Providence, RI 02908

Telephone: (401) 277-2172

SOUTH CAROLINA

Department: State Recruitment

Address: State of South Carolina
221 Devine Street, P.O. Box 50367
Columbia, SC 29250

Telephone: (803) 734-9085

SOUTH DAKOTA

Department:	Bureau of Personnel
Address:	State of South Dakota 500 E. Capitol Pierre, SD 57501-5070
Telephone:	(605) 773-4918 **Jobline: (605) 773-3326**

TENNESSEE

Department:	Department of Personnel
Address:	State of Tennessee Examination Division James K. Polk Building, 1st Floor 505 Deaderick St. Nashville, TN 37243
Telephone:	(615) 741-4841

TEXAS

Department:	Governor's Job Bank
Address:	State of Texas Sam Houston Building 201 E. 14th Austin, TX 78711
Telephone:	(512) 463-1792

UTAH

Department:	Department of Human Resource Management
Address:	State of Utah 2120 State Office Building Salt Lake City, UT 84114
Telephone:	(801) 538-3057

VERMONT

Department: Department of Personnel

Address: State of Vermont
110 State Street, Drawer 20
Montpelier, VT 05602

Telephone: (802) 828-3453   Jobline: (802) 828-3484

VIRGINIA

Department: Department of Personnel & Training

Address: State of Virginia
101 N. 14th St.
Richmond, VA 23219

Telephone: (804) 225-2131

WASHINGTON

Department: Department of Personnel

Address: State of Washington
600 South Franklin
Olympia, WA 98504

Joblines:
Olympic area: (206) 586-0545
Seattle area: (206) 464-7378
Spokane area: (509) 456-2889

Telephone: (206) 753-5368

WEST VIRIGINIA

Department: Division of Personnel

Address: State of West Virginia
5790A MacCorkle Ave. SE
Charleston, WV 25304

Telephone: (304) 558-5946

WISCONSIN

Department: Division of Merit Recruitment & Selection

Address: State of Wisconsin
P.O. Box 1855
137 E. Wilson St.
Madison, WI 55707-7855

Telephone: (608) 266-1731

WYOMING

Department: Personnel Management Division

Address: State of Wyoming
2001 Capitol Ave.
Emerson Building
Cheyenne, WY 82002-0060

Telephone: (307) 777-7188

COMPUTER DATABASES

The following section features the names and locations of governmental agencies that provide on-line computerized access to job and labor market information databases. All of the government bulletin boards can be accessed using a computer, a modem, and commercial or shareware communications software. Please note, you will be charged for all long-distance telephone charges when applicable.

DELAWARE DATALINE

WHAT YOU NEED

Computer
300, 1200 or 2400 speed modem
Telephone line
Communication software

COMMUNICATION SETTINGS

No parity
8 data bits
1 stop bit

BBS FEATURES

The Delaware Dataline bulletin board system provides up-to-date economic and demographic data for the state of Delaware. Information includes news, bulletins, economic and business analysis, wage and salary data, education and census reports.

Address

Delaware State Data Center
Delaware Development Office
99 Kings Highway
Dover, DE 19901

Data telephone

(302) 739-3757

Voice telephone

(302) 739-4271

FLORIDA LABOR MARKET INFORMATION NETWORK (LMI NET)

WHAT YOU NEED

Computer
300, 1200 or 2400 speed modem
Telephone line
Communication software

COMMUNICATION SETTINGS

No parity
8 data bits
1 stop bit
Emulation ANSI-BBS or
VT100, VT52

BBS FEATURES

Florida LMI NET is an on-line, menu-driven bulletin board system that allows users to access Bureau of Labor Market Information Resources. Data includes press releases, special labor reports, directories, economic data and analysis.

Address

Florida Dept. of Labor and
Employment Security
Division of Labor, Employment
and Training
Bureau of Labor Market Information
2012 Capital Circle, SE
200 Hartman Building
Tallahassee, FL 32399-2151

Data telephone

(904) 487-4187

Voice telephone

(904) 488-1048

IOWA DEPARTMENT OF EMPLOYMENT SERVICES DATALINE

WHAT YOU NEED

Computer
300, 1200 or 2400 speed modem
Telephone line
Communication software

COMMUNICATION SETTINGS

No parity
8 data bits
1 stop bit
Protocol: XModem
(recommended but optional)
Terminal: ANSI

BBS FEATURES

The DES Data Center is a communications system provided by the Iowa Department of Employment Services. The bulletin board system features full and part-time job openings statewide, economic and labor reports, news releases, directories and occupational data.

Address

Iowa Dept. of Employment Services
1000 East Grand Avenue
Des Moines, IA 50319

Data telephone

(515) 281-3472

Voice telephone

(515) 281-7307

LOUISIANA ELECTRONIC ASSISTANCE PROGRAM (LEAP)

WHAT YOU NEED

Computer
300, 1200 or 2400 speed modem
Telephone line
Communication software

COMMUNICATION SETTINGS

No parity
8 data bits
1 stop bit

BBS FEATURES

The Louisiana Electronic Assistance Program (LEAP) is a computerized bulletin board and database service that is designed to provide access to statewide business and economic information. Topics include wage and salary data, occupational and labor market reports, business and census data.

Address

Northeast Louisiana University
Center for Business & Economic
Research
Monroe, LA 71209-0101

Data telephone

(318) 342-5576

Voice telephone

(318) 342-1215

MONTANA BUSINESS INFORMATION

WHAT YOU NEED

Computer
300, 1200 or 2400 speed modem
Telephone line
Communication software

COMMUNICATION SETTINGS

No parity
8 data bits
1 stop bit

BBS FEATURES

Montana Business Information is a 24-hour electronic bulletin board system that features a wide variety of business, economic and demographic information that includes job service directories, wage and salary information, top employer listings, and various business directories.

Address

Montana Department of Commerce
Small Business Development Center
1424 Ninth Avenue
Helena, MT 59620

Data telephone

(406) 444-4457

Voice telephone

(406) 444-2463

NEBRASKA INFORMATION NETWORK & DATA EXCHANGE (Neb-Index)

WHAT YOU NEED

Computer
300, 1200 or 2400 speed modem
Telephone line
Communication software

COMMUNICATION SETTINGS

No parity
8 data bits
1 stop bit
VT100 Emulation

BBS FEATURES

Neb-Index is an on-line computerized bulletin board and database service for Nebraska. The bulletin board is designed to deliver state, county and local economic and business data. Information includes news releases, reports, resource materials and directories.

Address

Center for Public Affairs Research
University of Nebraska at Omaha
Omaha, NE 68182

Data telephone

(402) 595-2364

Voice telephone

(402) 595-2311

NEVADA ECONOMIC DATABASE SYSTEM

WHAT YOU NEED

Computer
300, 1200 or 2400 speed modem
Telephone line
Communication software

COMMUNICATION SETTINGS

No parity
8 data bits
1 stop bit

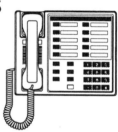

BBS FEATURES

The Research Section of the Nevada Employment Security Department bulletin board system features state and national labor market information. Examples of available information include occupational wage data, labor force and demographic information by county, industrial employment, and key information on state publications.

Address

Nevada Employment Security Dept.
Research Section
500 E. Third Street
Carson City, NV 89713

Data telephone

(702) 687-4194

Voice telephone

(702) 687-4550

OKLAHOMA (ORGINS)

WHAT YOU NEED

Computer
300, 1200 or 2400 speed modem
Telephone line
Communication software

COMMUNICATION SETTINGS

No parity
8 data bits
1 stop bit
Terminal Emulation: ANSI-BBS
or VT100, VT52

BBS FEATURES

Oklahoma ORGINS is an economic development information system containing current data on the state of Oklahoma. The computerized information service provides bulletins and databases of various economic and demographic data on state, counties and cities in Oklahoma. Database includes census data and labor market reports, venture capital and business directories.

Address

University of Oklahoma
Center for Economic & Management
Research (CEMR)
307 W. Brook Street
Room 4
Norman, OK 73019

Data telephone

(405) 325-5883

Voice telephone

(405) 841-5184

PENNSYLVANIA ECONOMIC DEVELOPMENT INFORMATION NETWORK (EDIN)

WHAT YOU NEED

Computer
300, 1200 or 2400 speed modem
Telephone line
Communication software

COMMUNICATION SETTINGS

Even Parity
7 data bits
1 start bit
1 stop bit
Full Duplex
Emulation: VT100

BBS FEATURES

The Pennsylvania Economic Development Information Network (EDIN) is an on-line, interactive database that contains thousands of items of information for Pennsylvania counties and municipalities. Information includes news releases, procurement opportunities, demographic and labor data, directories and small business assistance programs.

Address

Pennsylvania State Data Center
Penn State Harrisburg
Institute of State & Regional Affairs
Middletown, PA 17057-4898

Data telephone

(814) 863-0459 (1200 baud)
(814) 865-2424 (2400 baud)

Voice telephone

(717) 948-6336

UTAH LABOR MARKET INFORMATION

WHAT YOU NEED

Computer
300, 1200 or 2400 speed modem
Telephone line
Communication software

COMMUNICATION SETTINGS

No parity
8 data bits
1 stop bit

BBS FEATURES

The state of Utah is an electronic bulletin board system that features employment and wage data, occupations in demand, job and employment data for the entire Rocky Mountain region.

Address

State of Utah
Dept. of Employment Security
140 East 300 South
P.O. Box 11249
Salt Lake City, UT 84147-0249

Data telephone

(800) 828-5912

Voice telephone

(801) 536-7835

VERMONT EMPLOYMENT & TRAINING

WHAT YOU NEED

Computer
300, 1200 or 2400 speed modem
Telephone line
Communication software

COMMUNICATION SETTINGS

No parity
8 data bits
1 stop bit

BBS FEATURES

The Vermont Employment and Training is an electronic bulletin board that provides job opening bulletins and economic statistical data. The Job Opening Bulletins provide a condensed version of the job information available in the local state employment offices. The Economic Statistics Board features labor market data from the U.S. Bureau of Labor Statistics.

Address

State of Vermont
Vermont Dept. of Training
& Employment
P.O. Box 488
Montpelier, VT 05601-0488

Data telephone

(802) 828-4108

Voice telephone

(802) 828-4153

Career Communications, Inc. • P. O. Box 169 • Harleysville, PA 19438 • Telephone (215) 256-3130 • Fax (215) 256-3136

WASHINGTON STATE

WHAT YOU NEED

Computer
300, 1200 or 2400 speed modem
Telephone line
Communication software

COMMUNICATION SETTINGS

No parity
8 data bits
1 stop bit

BBS FEATURES

The Washington State Employment Security electronic bulletin board system provides labor market information to employers, governmental agencies, educators, researchers, and all other users of labor market information. Information includes wage and salary data, labor market news, hours and earnings, and a variety of labor market publications.

Address

Washington State Employment Security
Labor Market & Economic Analysis Branch
212 Maple Park MS:KG-11
Olympia, WA 98504-5311

Data telephone

(206) 438-3177

Voice telephone

(206) 438-4800

WEST VIRGINIA BUSINESS & ECONOMIC INFORMATION SYSTEM (WV-BEIS)

WHAT YOU NEED

Computer
300, 1200 or 2400 speed modem
Telephone line
Communication software

COMMUNICATION SETTINGS

No parity
8 data bits
1 stop bit

BBS FEATURES

WV-BEIS is a computerized bulletin board system that allows users to access a wide range of economic and demographic data for the state of West Virginia. Topics for state data include employment information, census data, economic forecasts and a county and city data book.

Address

West Virginia Business & Economic
Information System
Center for Economic Research
College of Business & Economics
West Virginia University
P. O. Box 6025
Morgantown, WV 26506-6025

Data telephone

(304) 293-6916

Voice telephone

(304) 293-7832

FEDERAL JOB OPPORTUNITIES BULLETIN BOARD – WASHINGTON, DC AREA

WHAT YOU NEED

Computer
300, 1200 or 2400 speed modem
Telephone line
Communication software

COMMUNICATION SETTINGS

No parity
8 data bits
1 stop bit
Full duplex

BBS FEATURES

The Office of Personnel Management's service center offers an electronic bulletin board service that lists nationwide government employment opportunities. You may scan current open examination and vacancy announcements while you're on-line or download them to your computer.

Address

U.S. Dept. of Personnel Management
Metropolitan Area
1900 E St. NW, Room 1416
Washington, DC 20415

Data telephone

(202) 606-1113

Voice telephone

(202) 606-2700

FEDERAL JOB OPPORTUNITIES BULLETIN BOARD – NORTH CENTRAL STATES

WHAT YOU NEED

Computer
300, 1200 or 2400 speed modem
Telephone line
Communication software

COMMUNICATION SETTINGS

No parity
8 data bits
1 stop bit
Full duplex

BBS FEATURES

The Office of Personnel Management's service center offers an electronic bulletin board service that lists nationwide government employment opportunities. You may scan current open examination and vacancy announcements while you're on-line or download them to your computer.

Address

U.S. Dept. of Personnel Management
Detroit Area Office
477 Michigan Ave., Room 565
Detroit, MI 48226-2574

Data telephone

(313) 226-4423

Voice telephone

(313) 226-6950

FEDERAL JOB OPPORTUNITIES BULLETIN BOARD – WESTERN STATES

WHAT YOU NEED

Computer
300, 1200 or 2400 speed modem
Telephone line
Communication software

COMMUNICATION SETTINGS

No parity
8 data bits
1 stop bit
Full duplex

BBS FEATURES

The Office of Personnel Management's service center offers an electronic bulletin board service that lists nationwide government employment opportunities. You may scan current open examination and vacancy announcements while you're on-line or download them to your computer.

Address

U.S. Dept. of Personnel Management
9650 Flair Drive
Suite 100A
El Monte, CA 91731

Data telephone

(818) 575-6521

Voice telephone

(818) 575-6510

FEDERAL JOB OPPORTUNITIES BULLETIN BOARD – NORTHEASTERN STATES

WHAT YOU NEED

Computer
300, 1200 or 2400 speed modem
Telephone line
Communication software

COMMUNICATION SETTINGS

No parity
8 data bits
1 stop bit
Full duplex

BBS FEATURES

The Office of Personnel Management's service center offers an electronic bulletin board service that lists nationwide government employment opportunities. You may scan current open examination and vacancy announcements while you're on-line or download them to your computer.

Address

U.S. Dept. of Personnel Management
Wm. J. Green, Jr. Federal Building
600 Arch Street
Philadelphia, PA 19106

Data telephone

(215) 580-2216

Voice telephone

(215) 597-7440

FEDERAL JOB OPPORTUNITIES BULLETIN BOARD – SOUTHEASTERN STATES

WHAT YOU NEED

Computer
300, 1200 or 2400 speed modem
Telephone line
Communication software

COMMUNICATION SETTINGS

No parity
8 data bits
1 stop bit
Full duplex

BBS FEATURES

The Office of Personnel Management's service center offers an electronic bulletin board service that lists nationwide government employment opportunities. You may scan current open examination and vacancy announcements while you're on-line or download them to your computer.

Address

U.S. Dept. of Personnel Management
Richard B. Russell Federal Building
Room 940A
75 Spring St., NW
Atlanta, GA 30303

Data telephone

(404) 730-2370

Voice telephone

(404) 331-4315

FEDERAL JOB OPPORTUNITIES BULLETIN BOARD – MOUNTAIN & SOUTHWESTERN STATES

WHAT YOU NEED

Computer
300, 1200 or 2400 speed modem
Telephone line
Communication software

COMMUNICATION SETTINGS

No parity
8 data bits
1 stop bit
Full duplex

BBS FEATURES

The Office of Personnel Management's service center offers an electronic bulletin board service that lists nationwide government employment opportunities. You may scan current open examination and vacancy announcements while you're on-line or download them to your computer.

Address

U.S. Dept. of Personnel Management
1100 Commerce Street
Room 6B10
Dallas, TX 75242

Data telephone

(214) 767-0316

Voice telephone

(214) 767-8035

Career Communications, Inc. • P. O. Box 169 • Harleysville, PA 19438 • Telephone (215) 256-3130 • Fax (215) 256-3136

NATIONAL CROSSWALK SERVICE CENTER (NCSC)

WHAT YOU NEED

Computer
300, 1200 or 2400 speed modem
Telephone line
Communication software

COMMUNICATION SETTINGS

No parity
8 data bits
1 stop bit
Full duplex

BBS FEATURES

The NCSC bulletin board system provides access to more than 90 occupational data files. Information resources include NOICC Master Crosswalks, BLS Crosswalks, SOC Career Profiles, SOC manual, military occupation and training data, occupational outlook handbook.

Address

National Crosswalk Service Center
Iowa SOICC
200 East Grand Ave.
Des Moines, IA 50309

Data telephone

(515) 242-4887

Voice telephone

(515) 242-4881

U.S. DEPARTMENT OF LABOR NEWS

WHAT YOU NEED

Computer
300, 1200 or 2400 speed modem
Telephone line
Communication software

COMMUNICATION SETTINGS

No parity
8 data bits
1 stop bit
Full duplex

BBS FEATURES

Labor News is an electronic bulletin board system that provides data briefs on job training grants, job safety and health developments, enforcement actions, new regulations, employment and unemployment statistics, news releases, fact sheets and selected labor publications.

Address

U.S Dept. of Labor
Office of Information & Public Affairs
Room S-1032
200 Constitution Ave. NW
Washington, DC 20210

Data telephone

(202) 219-4784

Voice telephone

(202) 219-7343

FEDERAL PERSONNEL OFFICES

The following section features an alphabetical listing of the names and locations of selected federal government agencies. Recorded jobline telephone numbers are listed where available.

ACTION

Department: Personnel Management

Address: 1100 Vermont Ave. NW, Room 5100
Washington, DC 20525

Telephone: (202) 606-5263   **Jobline:** (202) 606-5000

AGRICULTURE RESEARCH SERVICE

Department: Personnel Division

Address: 6303 Ivy Lane, Room 820
Greenbelt, MD 20770-1433

Telephone: (301) 344-1518   **Jobline:** (301) 344-2288

BUREAU OF CENSUS

Department: Personnel Division

Address: Room 1412
Federal Office Building #3
Washington, DC 20233

Telephone: (301) 763-7400   **Jobline:** (301) 763-6064

COMMERCE DEPARTMENT

Department: Office of Personnel

Address: Herbert C. Hoover Building
14th & Constitution Ave. NW
Washington, DC 20230

Telephone: (202) 482-2000

DEPARTMENT OF EDUCATION

Department: Personnel Office

Address: 400 Maryland Avenue SW
Washington, DC 20202

Telephone: (202) 401-0559

DEPARTMENT OF ENERGY

Department: Office of Personnel

Address: 1000 Independence Ave. SW
Washington, DC 20585

Telephone: (202) 586-8580   **Jobline:** (202) 586-4333

ENVIRONMENTAL PROTECTION AGENCY

Department: Employment Office

Address: 401 M Street SW
Washington, DC 20460

Telephone: (202) 260-2090   **Jobline:** (202) 260-5055

FEDERAL AVIATION ADMINISTRATION

Department: Employment Department

Address: 800 Independence Ave. SW
Washington, DC 20591

Telephone: (202) 267-3870   **Jobline:** (202) 267-8007

FEDERAL BUREAU OF INVESTIGATION

Department: Personnel Office

Address: 10th Street & Pennsylvania Ave. NW
Room 6329
Washington, DC 20535

Telephone: (202) 324-4991

FEDERAL TRADE COMMISSION

Department: Personnel Department

Address: Pennsylvania Ave. & 6th St. NW
Washington, DC 20580

Telephone: (202) 326-2022   **Jobline:** (202) 326-2020

FISH & WILDLIFE SERVICE

Department: Office of Personnel

Address: 4040 N. Fairfax Drive, Room 308
Arlington, VA 22203

Telephone: (703) 258-1743   **Jobline:** (703) 358-2120

FOOD AND DRUG ADMINISTRATION

Department: Personnel Office

Address: 5600 Fishers Lane, Room 7B-42
Rockville, MD 20857

Telephone: (301) 443-1970   **Jobline:** (301) 443-1969

GENERAL ACCOUNTING OFFICE

Department: Recruitment Office, Room 4043

Address: 441 G Street NW
Washington, DC 20548

Telephone: (202) 275-6092

GENERAL SERVICES ADMINISTRATION

Department: Office of Personnel

Address: National Capital Region
7th & D Sts. SW, WCPT Room 1019
Washington, DC 20407

Telephone: (202) 708-5300

HEALTH & HUMAN SERVICES

Department: Personnel Office

Address: Cohen Building, Room 1037
330 Independence Ave. SW
Washington, DC 20201

Telephone: (202) 619-0257   **Jobline:** (202) 619-2560

HOUSING & URBAN DEVELOPMENT

Department: Employment Office

Address: 451 7th Street SW
Room 2268
Washington, DC 20410

Telephone: (202) 708-0416   **Jobline:** (202) 708-3203

IMMIGRATION & NATURALIZATION SERVICE

Department: Employment Department

Address: 425 I St., NW
Room 6023
Washington, DC 20536

Telephone: (202) 514-2530   **Jobline:** (202) 514-4301

INTERIOR DEPT. –
MINERALS MANAGEMENT SERVICE

Department: Employment Office

Address: 381 Eldon St.
Herndon, VA 22070-4817

Telephone: (703) 787-1414   **Jobline:** (703) 787-1402

NASA GODDARD SPACE FLIGHT CENTER

Department: Personnel Department

Address: Code 115
Greenbelt, MD 20771

Telephone: (301) 286-7918   **Jobline:** (301) 286-5326

NAT'L ENDOWMENT FOR THE HUMANITIES

Department: Personnel Division

Address: 1100 Pennsylvania Avenue NW, Rm. 419
Washington, DC 20506

Telephone: (202) 606-8415   **Jobline:** (202) 606-8281

NATIONAL ARCHIVES & RECORDS ADMIN.

Department: Personnel Services Division

Address: 7th & Pennsylvania Ave. NW
Washington, DC 20408

Telephone: (202) 501-6100

NATIONAL ENDOWMENT FOR THE ARTS

Department: Personnel Division

Address: 1100 Pennsylvania Avenue NW, Rm. 208
Washington, DC 20506

Telephone: (202) 682-5799

NATIONAL INSTITUTE OF HEALTH

Department: Personnel Office

Address: Building No. 31, Rm. 83C15
9000 Rockville Pike
Bethesda, MD 20892

Telephone: (301) 496-2404   **Jobline: (301) 496-2403**

NATIONAL INSTITUTE OF STANDARDS & TECHNOLOGY

Department: Office of Personnel

Address: Administration Building 101, Room A123
Gaithersburg, MD 20899

Telephone: (301) 975-3007   **Jobline: (301) 926-4851**

NATIONAL PARK SERVICE

Department: Personnel Department

Address: 1100 Ohio Drive SW, Room 244
Washington, DC 20242

Telephone: (202) 619-7256   **Jobline:** (202) 619-7111

NATIONAL SCIENCE FOUNDATION

Department: Office of Personnel

Address: 1800 G Street, NW
Room 208
Washington, DC 20550

Telephone: (202) 357-7602   **Jobline:** (202) 357-7735

PATENT AND TRADEMARK OFFICE

Department: Office of Personnel

Address: 2011 Crystal Drive, Box 171
Washington, DC 20231

Telephone: (703) 557-3158

PEACE CORPS

Department: Office of Personnel

Address: 1990 K Street NW, Suite 4100
Washington, DC 20526

Telephone: (202) 606-3336   **Jobline:** (202) 606-3214

SMITHSONIAN INSTITUTE

Department: Personnel Department

Address: 955 L'Enfant Plaza SW
Suite 2100
Washington, DC 20560

Telephone: (202) 287-3100   **Jobline:** (202) 287-3102

STATE DEPARTMENT

Department: Employment Information Office

Address: 2201 C Street
Washington, DC 20520

Telephone: (202) 647-7284   **Jobline:** (202) 647-7284

US GEOLOGICAL SURVEY

Department: Personnel Office

Address: 12201 Sunrise Valley Drive , MS-215
Reston, VA 22092

Telephone: (703) 648-6131   **Jobline:** (703) 648-7676

US INFORMATION AGENCY

Department: Human Resources

Address: 301 4th Street SW, Room 518
Washington, DC 20547

Telephone: (202) 619-4659   **Jobline:** (202) 619-4539

USDA FOREST SERVICE PERSONNEL MGMT.

Department: Personnel Division

Address: P.O. Box 96090
                Room 913 - (RPE)
                Washington, DC 20090

Telephone: (703) 235-8102   Jobline: (703) 235-JOBS

VETERANS AFFAIRS MEDICAL CENTER

Department: Personnel Office

Address: 50 Irving Street, NW
                Washington, DC 20422

Telephone: (202) 745-8204

VOICE OF AMERICA

Department: Personnel Department

Address: 330 Independence Ave. SW, Room 1543
                Washington, DC 20547

Telephone: (202) 619-376   Jobline: (202) 619-0909

WALTER REED ARMY MEDICAL CENTER

Department: Personnel Division

Address: CPO (JIC), Bldg. 11, Room 1-131
                6825 16th Street NW
                Washington, DC 20307-5001

Telephone: (202) 576-0546

FEDERAL PUBLICATIONS

The following section features selected job, career and labor market publications available from the U.S. Government Printing Office. To order any of the publications, please use the order form found on page 104 or contact the Superintendent of Documents.

ADMINISTRATIVE CAREERS WITH AMERICA

Description: Prepared especially for college seniors. Discusses how to apply for entry level jobs in the Federal government. 1991: 7 p. Sold in Packages of 50 only. S/N 006-000-01350-3. $27.00.

Address: Superintendent of Documents
United States Government Printing Office
Washington, DC 20402

Telephone: (202) 783-3238

AMERICANS WITH DISABILITIES ACT HANDBOOK

Description: Provides information and assistance to people with disabilities, businesses, and the affected public. The Act provides the following for disabled people: equal employment opportunity; nondiscrimination in public accomodations; and access to State and local government services. 1991: 716 p.; ill. looseleaf. S/N 052-015-00072-3. $30.00.

Address: Superintendent of Documents
United States Government Printing Office
Washington, DC 20402

Telephone: (202) 783-3238

AMERICANS WITH DISABILITIES ACT OF 1990, PUBLIC LAW 101-336

Description: An Act to Establish a Clear and Comprehensive Prohibition of Discrimination on the Basis of Disability. Approved July 26, 1990. 1990: 51 p. S/N 869-010-00096-1. $1.50.

Address: Superintendent of Documents
United States Government Printing Office
Washington, DC 20402

Telephone: (202) 783-3238

AMERICANS WITH DISABILITIES ACT
TECHNICAL ASSISTANCE MANUAL

Description: Subscription service consists of a basic manual with supplementary material for an indeterminate period. In looseleaf form, punched for 3-ring binder. Designed to help employers, other covered entities, and persons with disabilities learn about their obligations and rights under Public Law 101-336. Also provides a directory of resources to aid in compliance, and guidance on the practical application of legal requirements established in the statute and EEOC compliance. Subscription price: Domestic - $25.00; Foreign - $31.25. S/N 952-020-00000-5.

Address: Superintendent of Documents
United States Government Printing Office
Washington, DC 20402

Telephone: (202) 783-3238

BALANCING WORK RESPONSIBILITIES AND FAMILY NEEDS:
THE FEDERAL CIVIL SERVICE RESPONSE

Description: Discusses child care, elder care, alternative work schedules, part-time employment, flexiplace, leave-sharing programs, "cafeteria" benefits, emerging benefit areas, OPM program leadership, and policy issues. 1991: 106 p.; ill. S/N 062-000-00028-7. $6.00.

Address: Superintendent of Documents
United States Government Printing Office
Washington, DC 20402

Telephone: (202) 783-3238

BEA REGIONAL PROJECTIONS TO 2040: VOLUME 1: STATES

Description: Presents projections to 2040 of economic activity and population for the Nation and the States. Provides projections for: population in three age groups; personal income, classified by major income component; and employment and earnings, each of which is presented for 57 industrial groups. Shows projections for 1995, 2000, 2005, 2010, 2020, and 2040. Gives historical data for 1973, 1979, 1983, and 1988. 1990:144 p. S/N 003-010-00199-2. $7.50.

Address: Superintendent of Documents
United States Government Printing Office
Washington, DC 20402

Telephone: (202) 783-3238

BEA REGIONAL PROJECTIONS TO 2040: VOLUME 2: METROPOLITAN STATISTICAL AREAS

Description: Presents projections for metropolitan areas for employment by industry, earnings, total personal income, and population for 1995 through 2040. Appendices include metropolitan statistical area classifications and industrial classifications. 1990: 352 p. S/N 003-010-00211-5. $17.00.

Address: Superintendent of Documents
United States Government Printing Office
Washington, DC 20402

Telephone: (202) 783-3238

BEA REGIONAL PROJECTIONS TO 2040: VOLUME 3: BEA ECONOMIC AREAS

Description: Presents projections to the year 2040 of economic activity and population projections for Bureau of Economic Analysis economic areas and the Nation. Appendices include an economic area definition and industrial classifications. 1990: 199 p. S/N 003-010-00212-3. $10.00.

Address: Superintendent of Documents United States Government Printing Office Washington, DC 20402

Telephone: (202) 783-3238

BOTTOM LINE: BASIC SKILLS IN THE WORKPLACE

Description: Discusses how to set up literacy and skills enhancement programs at work. Includes a bibliography and the addresses of organizations that are concerned about adult literacy and education. 1988: 56 p.; ill. S/N 029-000-00424-2. $3.25.

Address: Superintendent of Documents United States Government Printing Office Washington, DC 20402

Telephone: (202) 783-3238

BUILDING A QUALITY WORKFORCE

Description: Suggests that businesses and schools need to work together to help entry level workers be better prepared for employment. States that the basic skills gap between what business needs and the qualifications of the entry level workers available to business is widening. Also discusses community partnerships that have worked in Prince Georges County, Maryland, Cincinnati, Ohio, and Portland, Oregon. 1988: 85 p. S/N 029-000-00425-1. $4.50.

Address: Superintendent of Documents United States Government Printing Office Washington, DC 20402

Telephone: (202) 783-3238

CAREER AMERICA (PORTFOLIO)

Description: Portfolio contains eight brochures: Welcome to Career America; Employment Facts at a Glance; Career America: The Challenge, the Opportunity, the United States Government (College Recruiting); Cooperative Education; Student Employment Programs; Job Opportunities for Persons With Disabilities; Job Opportunities for Veterans; and Presidential Management Internships. Provides information about working for the United States Government. 1988: Portfolio of 8 folders. S/N 006-000-01328-7. $7.5O.

Address: Superintendent of Documents
United States Government Printing Office
Washington, DC 20402

Telephone: (202) 783-3238

CAREER AMERICA: THE CHALLENGE, THE OPPORTUNITY, THE UNITED STATES GOVERNMENT (COLLEGE RECRUITING)

Description: Single brochure of Career America Portfolio. Includes information on: the Challenge of Career with America; opportunity for excellence; paths to advancement; cooperative education program; wanted: skills, knowledge, dedication, and vision; presidential management intern program; Career America: The Next Step; and other related information. 1988: 13 p. Sold in Packages of 50 only.
S/N 006-000-01330-9. $27.00.

Address: Superintendent of Documents
United States Government Printing Office
Washington, DC 20402

Telephone: (202) 783-3238

CAREER AMERICA: COOPERATIVE EDUCATION

Description: Single brochure of Career America Portfolio. Includes information on: the Federal Cooperative Education Program; occupations and locations; pay and benefits; and other related information. 1988: Folder. Sold in Packages of 50 only. S/N 006-000-01334-1. $11.00.

Address: Superintendent of Documents
United States Government Printing Office
Washington, DC 20402

Telephone: (202) 783-3238

CAREER AMERICA: EMPLOYMENT FACTS AT A GLANCE

Description: Single brochure of Career America Portfolio. Includes information on: sources for getting a Federal job; health benefits and insurance; and other related information. 1988: 5 p. Sold in Packages of 50 only. S/N 006-000-01329-5. $5.50.

Address: Superintendent of Documents
United States Government Printing Office
Washington, DC 20402

Telephone: (202) 783-3238

CAREER AMERICA: JOB OPPORTUNITIES FOR PERSONS WITH DISABILITIES

Description: Single brochure of Career America Portfolio. Includes information on: opportunities for persons with disabilities; selective placement procedures; special accommodations on the job; and other related information. 1988: Folder. Sold in Packages of 50 only. S/N 006-000-01331-7. $11.00.

Address: Superintendent of Documents
United States Government Printing Office
Washington, DC 20402

Telephone: (202) 783-3238

CAREER AMERICA: JOB OPPORTUNITIES FOR VETERANS

Description: Single brochure of Career America Portfolio. Includes information on: job opportunities for veterans; Federal employee benefits package; Veterans Readjustment Appointment (VRA) Hiring Authority program; hiring for severely disabled veterans; and other related information. 1988: Folder. Sold in Packages of 50 only. S/N 006-000-01332-5. $11.00.

Address: Superintendent of Documents
United States Government Printing Office
Washington, DC 20402

Telephone: (202) 783-3238

CAREER AMERICA: PRESIDENTIAL MANAGEMENT INTERNSHIPS

Description: Single brochure of Career America Portfolio. Includes information on: the Presidential Management Intern Program; career in public policies and programs; advancement; and other related information. 1988: Folder. Sold in Packages of 50 only. S/N 006-000-01335-0. $11.00.

Address: Superintendent of Documents
United States Government Printing Office
Washington, DC 20402

Telephone: (202) 783-3238

CAREER AMERICA: STUDENT EMPLOYMENT PROGRAMS

Description: Single brochure of Career America Portfolio. Includes information on: the Federal Junior Fellowship program; Stay-in-School program; Summer Employment program; Student Volunteer services; and other related information. 1988: Folder. Sold in Packages of 50 only. S/N 006-000-01333-3. $11.00.

Address: Superintendent of Documents
United States Government Printing Office
Washington, DC 20402

Telephone: (202) 783-3238

CENSUS OF POPULATION AND HOUSING, 1990, CLASSIFIED INDEX OF INDUSTRIES AND OCCUPATIONS

Description: Provides a comprehensive list of 21,000 industries and 30,000 occupational titles which have been developed over time, and continuously updated through review of census and survey questionnaires. 1992: 291 p. S/N 003-024-08081-8. $14.00.

Address: Superintendent of Documents
United States Government Printing Office
Washington, DC 20402

Telephone: (202) 783-3238

CIVIL SERVICE 2000

Description: Outlines the expected demographic changes in the Federal workforce and the changes in skills that the government will need between now and the year 2000. Includes an appendix which discusses Federal child care programs and policies. 1988: 54 p. S/N 006-000-01337-6. $2.50.

Address: Superintendent of Documents
United States Government Printing Office
Washington, DC 20402

Telephone: (202) 783-3238

CIVIL SERVICE REFORM ACT OF 1978, PUBLIC LAW 95-454

Description: An Act to Reform the Civil Service Laws. Approved October 13, 1978. 1978: 117 p. S/N 022-003-91985-6. $4.25.

Address: Superintendent of Documents
United States Government Printing Office
Washington, DC 20402

Telephone: (202) 783-3238

COMPARISON OF STATE UNEMPLOYMENT INSURANCE LAWS 1991.

Description: Subscription service consists of a basic manual and supplementary material for an indeterminate period. A series of semiannual revisions reflecting changes in State unemployment insurance laws. Subscription price: Domestic - $45.00; Foreign - $56.25. S/N 929-002-00000-8.

Address: Superintendent of Documents
United States Government Printing Office
Washington, DC 20402

Telephone: (202) 783-3238

COUNTY GOVERNMENT EMPLOYMENT: 1990

Description: Provides national statistics on county government and payrolls for the month of October 1990. Based on a mail canvass survey that includes a sample of 2,026 county governments. 1991: 44 p. S/N 003-024-07290-4. $2.50.

Address: Superintendent of Documents
United States Government Printing Office
Washington, DC 20402

Telephone: (202) 783-3238

CRIMINAL JUSTICE CAREERS GUIDEBOOK

Description: Most of this book is comprised of individual criminal justice career descriptions; each of these includes information about job requirements and employment prospects. Also includes a bibliography and a list of sources to contact for further information. 1982: 184 p.; ill. 1987-repr. S/N 029-014-00200-3. $7.00.

Address: Superintendent of Documents
United States Government Printing Office
Washington, DC 20402

Telephone: (202) 783-3238

DICTIONARY OF OCCUPATIONAL TITLES

Description: Defines and indexes over 20,000 job titles. Addresses issues of training and education, career guidance and employment counseling, job definition and wage restructuring. This publication may be purchased at a "warehouse" price of $24.60. 1991: 2 bks. (1445 p.); revised ed. S/N 029-013-00094-2. $40.00.

Address: Superintendent of Documents
United States Government Printing Office
Washington, DC 20402

Telephone: (202) 783-3238

DIRECTORY OF NONTRADITIONAL TRAINING AND EMPLOYMENT PROGRAMS SERVING WOMEN

Description: Provides information on 125 programs and services for women seeking jobs in trades and technology. The programs are divided according to those that primarily focus on: training, information and technical assistance, and outreach. Also includes appendices. 1991: 165 p. S/N 029-002-00080-1. $9.00.

Address: Superintendent of Documents
United States Government Printing Office
Washington, DC 20402

Telephone: (202) 783-3238

DISPLACED WORKERS, 1985-89

Description: Discusses the plight of workers displaced from their jobs because of plant closings or employment cutbacks from January 1985 through January 1990. 1991: 38 p. S/N 029-001-03080-1. $2.25.

Address: Superintendent of Documents
United States Government Printing Office
Washington, DC 20402

Telephone: (202) 783-3238

EMERGENCY UNEMPLOYMENT COMPENSATION ACT OF 1991, PUBLIC LAW 102-164

Description: An Act to provide a Program of Emergency Unemployment Compensation, and for Other Purposes. Approved November 15, 1991. 1991: 21 p. S/N 869-015-00164-1. $1.00.

Address: Superintendent of Documents
United States Government Printing Office
Washington, DC 20402

Telephone: (202) 783-3238

EMPLOYMENT AND EARNINGS

Description: (Monthly and Annual Supplement.) Subscription service will be accepted for one or two years. Current data on employment, hours, and earnings for the United States as a whole, for States, and for more than 200 local areas. Supplement presents revised data for recent years from the survey of business establishments. Subscription price: Domestic - $31.00 a year; Foreign - $38.75 a year. Single copy price: Domestic - $10.00 a copy; Foreign - $12.50 a copy. Annual Supplement: Domestic - $11.00 a copy; Foreign - $13. 75 a copy. S/N 729-004-00000-6.

Address: Superintendent of Documents
United States Government Printing Office
Washington, DC 20402

Telephone: (202) 783-3238

EMPLOYMENT AND WAGES ANNUAL AVERAGES, 1990

Description: Presents 1990 annual data on employment and wages based on the 1987 Standard Industrial Classification Manual. The data relate to workers covered by Unemployment Insurance (UI) laws and Federal civilian workers covered by the Unemployment Compensation of Federal Employees (UCFE) program. The data for both private and public workers are reported to BLS by the employment security agencies of the 50 States and the District of Columbia. 1991: 540 p.; ill. S/N 029-001-03088-6. $27.00.

Address: Superintendent of Documents
United States Government Printing Office
Washington, DC 20402

Telephone: (202) 783-3238

EMPLOYMENT COST INDEXES AND LEVELS, 1975-91

Description: Provides data on two BLS measures of employee compensation: the Employment Cost Index (ECI) and Employer Costs for Employee Compensation. Both measures are based on data collected in the same sample survey of establishments, but are computed with different sets of employment weights. 1991: 140 p.; ill. S/N 029-001-03089-4. $7.50.

Address: Superintendent of Documents
United States Government Printing Office
Washington, DC 20402

Telephone: (202) 783-3238

EMPLOYMENT, HOURS, AND EARNINGS, UNITED STATES: 1909-1990, VOLUMES 1-2

Description: Presents monthly and annual average data on national establishment-based employment, hours, and earnings by detailed industry based on the 1987 Standard Industrial Classification structure. Volume 1 presents data for goods-producing industries; Volume 2, service-producing industries. 1991: 2 bks. (1050 p.) S/N 029-001-03075-4. $31.00.

Address: Superintendent of Documents
United States Government Printing Office
Washington, DC 20402

Telephone: (202) 783-3238

ERGONOMICS: THE STUDY OF WORK

Description: Discusses the types of work patterns that may cause Cumulative Trauma Disorders (CTDs) and other musculoskeletal or nervous system disorders resulting from ergonomic hazards, and the methods employers can use to control or prevent their occurrence. The term "ergonomics" can simply be defined as the study of work. Ergonomics helps adapt the job to fit the person, rather than forces the person to fit the job. Also includes references, bibliography, and States with approved plans. 1991: 28 p.; ill. S/N 029-016-00124-7. $1.00.

Address: Superintendent of Documents
United States Government Printing Office
Washington, DC 20402

Telephone: (202) 783-3238

FEDERAL CAREER DIRECTORY: THE UNITED STATES GOVERNMENT, CAREER AMERICA

Description: Prepared especially for guidance counselors, recent college graduates, students, Federal employees, and people who are interested in working for the Federal government. Provides information about Federal employment and career opportunities. Much of the book is an alphabetical directory of Federal government departments and agencies, with information about employment, and addresses and telephone numbers of personnel offices. 1990: 271 p.; ill. looseleaf and binder. S/N 006-000-01339-2. $31.00.

Address: Superintendent of Documents
United States Government Printing Office
Washington, DC 20402

Telephone: (202) 783-3238

FEDERAL PERSONNEL MANUAL SUPPLEMENT 298-2

Description: The 113 Summary Data Reporting System. Subscription service consists of a basic manual and supplementary material issued irregularly for an indeterminate period. In looseleaf form, punched for 3-ring binder. Subscription price: Domestic - $41.00; Foreign - $51.25. S/N 906-008-00000-9.

Address: Superintendent of Documents
United States Government Printing Office
Washington, DC 20402

Telephone: (202) 783-3238

FEDERAL STAFFING DIGEST

Description: (Quarterly.) Describes current activities and programs in the area of recruiting, college recruiting, and affirmative employment. Subscription price: Domestic - $6.50 a year; Foreign - $8.15 a year. Single copy price: Domestic - $1.75 a copy; Foreign - $2.19 a copy. S/N 706-004-00000-9.

Address: Superintendent of Documents
United States Government Printing Office
Washington, DC 20402

Telephone: (202) 783-3238

GEOGRAPHIC PROFILE OF EMPLOYMENT AND UNEMPLOYMENT, 1991,1992

Description: 163 p.; ill. S/N 029-001-03125-4. $10.00.

Address: Superintendent of Documents
United States Government Printing Office
Washington, DC 20402

Telephone: (202) 783-3238

GUIDE TO SENIOR EXECUTIVE SERVICE QUALIFICATIONS, 1991, 1992

Description: 16 p.; ill. S/N 006-000-01375-9. $2.25.

Address: Superintendent of Documents
United States Government Printing Office
Washington, DC 20402

Telephone: (202) 783-3238

HANDBOOK OF OCCUPATIONAL GROUPS AND SERIES

Description: Intended for Federal agencies as an aid to classifying positions under the Classification Act of 1949. Organized by General Schedule occupational group number. Indexed alphabetically by occupation. 1991: 70 p. S/N 006-000-01360-1. $4.00.

Address: Superintendent of Documents
United States Government Printing Office
Washington, DC 20402

Telephone: (202) 783-3238

HANDBOOK X-118: QUALIFICATION STANDARDS FOR POSITIONS UNDER THE GENERAL SCHEDULE 1989

Description: Consolidated reprint. Subscription service consists of the Handbook, reprinted to incorporate changes through Transmittal Sheet 229, and monthly revised pages for an indeterminate period. In looseleaf form, punched for 3-ring binder. Furnishes current qualification standards for various grade-level occupations in the Office of Personnel Management, under the Classification Act of 1949. Subscription price: Domestic - $114.00; Foreign - $142.50. S/N 906-030-00000-4.

Address: Superintendent of Documents
United States Government Printing Office
Washington, DC 20402

Telephone: (202) 783-3238

INVESTING IN PEOPLE: STRATEGY TO ADDRESS AMERICA'S WORKFORCE CRISIS, A REPORT TO THE SECRETARY OF LABOR AND THE AMERICAN PEOPLE

Description: Suggests ways to improve America's workforce and the quality of work in the Nation. Includes sections on: the foundation of workforce quality; lifetime education and training; putting quality to work; and understanding the workforce. 1989:73p.
S/N 029-000-00428-5. $3.75.

Address: Superintendent of Documents
United States Government Printing Office
Washington, DC 20402

Telephone: (202) 783-3238

JOB CREATION DURING THE LATE 1980s: DYNAMIC ASPECTS OF EMPLOYMENT GROWTH

Description: Provides data on persons with job accessions during the life of the 1987 SIPP panel. In this report, a job accession is defined as not have a job one month but having a job the following month. 1992: 29 p.; ill.
S/N 803-044-00015-5. $1.75.

Address: Superintendent of Documents
United States Government Printing Office
Washington, DC 20402

Telephone: (202) 783-3238

JOB DIRECTIONS, A GUIDE TO EMPLOYMENT AND TRAINING PROGRAMS

Description: Briefly answers such questions as: Do you need help looking for work?; Do you want to apply for unemployment insurance benefits?; Are you looking for training to improve your job skills?; Are you a young person looking to make a new life for yourself?; Do you want to learn a skilled trade?; Are you out of work?; and Are you a senior citizen? Also lists the ETA Regional Offices. 1991: 8p.; ill. Sold in packages of 100 only. S/N 029-014-00245-3. $41.00.

Address: Superintendent of Documents
United States Government Printing Office
Washington, DC 20402

Telephone: (202) 783-3238

JOB GRADING SYSTEM FOR TRADES AND LABOR OCCUPATIONS

Description: 1992, Consolidated reprint. Subscription service consists of 3 parts. Part 1 contains basic information relating to the subscription service; part 2 contains a description of the Individual Job Standards; and part 3 contains occupational definitions. Subscription price: Domestic - $69.00; Foreign - $86.25.
S/N 906-031-00000-1.

Address: Superintendent of Documents
United States Government Printing Office
Washington, DC 20402

Telephone: (202) 783-3238

JOB OUTLOOK IN BRIEF, 1990-2005

Description: Provides thumbnail sketches of employment data for each of the occupations in the 1992-93 edition of the "Occupational Outlook Handbook." Each entry presents the occupation's title, its 1990 employment, the present change projected in employment between 1990 and 2005, the projected numerical change, and a summary of job prospects. 1992: 36 p. (6-41 p.); ill. S/N 029-001-03124-6. $2.25.

Address: Superintendent of Documents
United States Government Printing Office
Washington, DC 20402

Telephone: (202) 783-3238

JOB PATTERNS FOR MINORITIES AND WOMEN IN PRIVATE INDUSTRY, 1989

Description: Consists chiefly of tables and statistics. Based on information from "Employer Information Report (EEO-1), Standard Form 100" which private employers filed with the Equal Employment Opportunity Commission. 1990: 697 p. S/N 052-015-00070-7. $30.00.

Address: Superintendent of Documents
United States Government Printing Office
Washington, DC 20402

Telephone: (202) 783-3238

LEARNING A LIVING: A BLUEPRINT FOR HIGH PERFORMANCE, A SCANS REPORT FOR AMERICA 2000: PART 1

Description: Describes the economic choices facing the United States, defines the workforce issues to be understood, and makes several recommendations to set the nation on the path to a high-performance future. 1992: 40 p.; ill. S/N 029-000-00439-1. $2.50.

Address: Superintendent of Documents
United States Government Printing Office
Washington, DC 20402

Telephone: (202) 783-3238

LEARNING A LIVING: A BLUEPRINT FOR HIGH PERFORMANCE, A SCANS REPORT FOR AMERICA 2000: PART 2, FINAL REPORT

Description: Provides a more detailed roadmap for those charged with the responsibility for the Commission's major concerns: educators, employers, and the designers of our certification and assessment systems. 1992: 108 p.; ill. S/N 029-000-00440-4. $6.50.

Address: Superintendent of Documents
United States Government Printing Office
Washington, DC 20402

Telephone: (202) 783-3238

MATCHING YOURSELF WITH THE WORLD OF WORK

Description: Lists and defines 17 occupational characteristics and requirements. Matches these characteristics with 200 occupations chosen from the Occupational Outlook Handbook, 1986-87 Edition. 1986: 10 p.; ill. 1991 -repr. S/N 029-001-02910-1. $1.00.

Address: Superintendent of Documents
United States Government Printing Office
Washington, DC 20402

Telephone: (202) 783-3238

MONTHLY LABOR REVIEW

Description: Subscription service will be accepted for one or two years. Articles on labor force, wages, prices, productivity, economic growth, and occupational injuries and illnesses. Regular features include a review of developments in industrial relations, book reviews, and current labor statistics. Subscription price: Domestic - $22.00 a year; Foreign - $27.50 a year. Single copy price: Domestic - $5.00 a copy; Foreign - $6.25 a copy. S/N 729-007-00000-5.

Address: Superintendent of Documents
United States Government Printing Office
Washington, DC 20402

Telephone: (202) 783-3238

OCCUPATIONAL OUTLOOK HANDBOOK, 1992-1993 EDITION

Description: Describes what workers do on each job, the training and education they need, earnings, working conditions, and expected job prospects on about 200 occupations. Cloth: This publication may be purchased at a "warehouse" price of $17.10. 1992: 481 p.; ill. S/N 029-001-03090-8. $26.00. Paper: This publication may be purchased at a "warehouse" price of $14.85. 1992: 481 p.; ill. S/N 029-001-03091-6. $23.00. Collated Set of Reprints from the above: Includes 20 booklets of information reprinted from the Occupational Outlook Handbook, 1992-1993 Edition. This publication may be purchased at a "warehouse" price of $15.60. 1992: 20 bks. (465 p.) S/N 029-001-03092-4. $24.00.

Address: Superintendent of Documents
United States Government Printing Office
Washington, DC 20402

Telephone: (202) 783-3238

OCCUPATIONAL PROJECTIONS AND TRAINING DATA: 1992 EDITION

Description: Provides detailed statistics used in preparing the Occupational Outlook Handbook and reports on research that improves occupational information. 1992: 97 p. S/N 029-001-03123-8. $5.50.

Address: Superintendent of Documents
United States Government Printing Office
Washington, DC 20402

Telephone: (202) 783-3238

OCCUPATIONAL OUTLOOK QUARTERLY

Description: Subscription service will be accepted for one or two years. A periodical to help young people, employment planners, and guidance counselors keep abreast of current occupational and employment developments. The Quarterly, written in nontechnical language and illustrated in color, contains articles on new occupations, training opportunities, salary trends, career counseling programs, and the results of new studies from the Bureau of Labor Statistics. Subscription price: Domestic - $6.50 a year; Foreign-$8.15 a year. Single copy price: Domestic - $2.50 a copy; Foreign - $3.13 a copy. S/N 729-008-00000-1.

Address: Superintendent of Documents
United States Government Printing Office
Washington, DC 20402

Telephone: (202) 783-3238

OPPORTUNITY 2000: CREATIVE AFFIRMATIVE ACTION STRATEGIES FOR A CHANGING WORKFORCE

Description: Includes sections on: the American labor market's emerging challenges; work and families; minorities and the economically disadvantaged; disabled workers; workers with AIDS; older workers; veterans in the civilian workforce; and a human resources approach to affirmative action. 1988: 195 p.
S/N 029-014-00242-9. $5.00.

Address: Superintendent of Documents
United States Government Printing Office
Washington, DC 20402

Telephone: (202) 783-3238

OUTLOOK 1990-2005

Description: Presents Bureau of Labor Statistics employment projections for the year 2005. Includes five articles reprinted from the November 1991 "Monthly Labor Review," a brief review of the methodology, the assumptions underlying the specific industry and occupational employment estimates. 1992: 150p.; ill. S/N 029-001-03120-3. $8.50.

Address: Superintendent of Documents
United States Government Printing Office
Washington, DC 20402

Telephone: (202) 783-3238

OUTLOOK FOR TECHNOLOGY AND LABOR IN HOSPITALS

Description: Discusses the major technological changes that are emerging in hospitals. Consists of tables, charts, and selected bibliography. 1992: 23 p.; ill. S/N 029-001-03122-0. $2.25.

Address: Superintendent of Documents
United States Government Printing Office
Washington, DC 20402

Telephone: (202) 783-3238

PERFORMANCE STANDARDS FOR THE FOOD STAMP EMPLOYMENT AND TRAINING PROGRAM

Description: Reports on the proposed performance standards for the Food Stamp Employment and Training Program (FSET), and examines the implementation of these standards to meet the goal to reduce food stamp outlays by increasing the employment and earnings of able-bodied food stamp recipients. 1992: 40 p. S/N 052-003-01276-6. $2.25.

Address: Superintendent of Documents
United States Government Printing Office
Washington, DC 20402

Telephone: (202) 783-3238

PERSONNEL RESEARCH HIGHLIGHTS SPECIAL REPORT ON THE SUMMARY OF FEDERAL EMPLOYEES, 1992

Description: 1992: 67 p.; ill. S/N 006-000-01373-2. $4.50.

Address: Superintendent of Documents
United States Government Printing Office
Washington, DC 20402

Telephone: (202) 783-3238

PIPELINES OF PROGRESS: AN UPDATE ON THE GLASS CEILING INITIATIVE

Description: A report on what is taking place in America to ensure that artificial barriers are broken so that merit can determine the career advancement of talented minorities and women. 1992: 45 p.; ill. S/N 029-016-00141-7. $3.25.

Address: Superintendent of Documents
United States Government Printing Office
Washington, DC 20402

Telephone: (202) 783-3238

PUBLIC EMPLOYMENT: 1991

Description: 1992: 48 p. S/N 003-024-08573-9. $3.25.

Address: Superintendent of Documents
United States Government Printing Office
Washington, DC 20402

Telephone: (202) 783-3238

REPORT ON THE GLASS CEILING INITIATIVE

Description: Discusses pilot studies of the hiring and promotion practices of nine major corporations. Glass ceilings are defined as those artificial barriers based on attitudinal or organizational bias that prevent qualified individuals from advancing upward in their organization into management level positions. 1991: 29 p. S/N 029-016-00135-2. $3.25.

Address: Superintendent of Documents
United States Government Printing Office
Washington, DC 20402

Telephone: (202) 783-3238

RESUMES, APPLICATION FORMS, COVER LETTERS, AND INTERVIEWS

Description: Briefly describes how to create effective resumes and application forms and how to succeed at taking tests and facing interviews. 1987: 7 p.; ill.
S/N 029-001-02926-8. $1.00.

Address: Superintendent of Documents
United States Government Printing Office
Washington, DC 20402

Telephone: (202) 783-3238

REVISED HANDBOOK FOR ANALYZING JOBS

Description: This manual explains the procedures and techniques used in the public employment service to analyze jobs and record the analyses. These procedures were developed to meet the occupational information needs of various human resource programs, and are applicable to any job analysis program, regardless of the intended utilization of the data. 1991: 239 p. revised ed. S/N 029-013-00095-1. $12.00.

Address: Superintendent of Documents
United States Government Printing Office
Washington, DC 20402

Telephone: (202) 783-3238

SENIOR EXECUTIVE SERVICE

Description: Provides a general description of the Senior Executive Service of the Federal government, what it is, and how it works. Includes sections on: positions and appointments; compensations, benefits, and awards; career development and advancement; performance management; removal; and protection against arbitrary actions. 1991: 21 p.; ill. S/N 006-000-01354-6. $2.00.

Address: Superintendent of Documents
United States Government Printing Office
Washington, DC 20402

Telephone: (202) 783-3238

SKILLS AND TASKS FOR JOBS: A SCANS REPORT OF AMERICA 2000

Description: Designed to help educators make high school courses more relevant to the needs of a modern workforce and to help employers ensure that their employees possess appropriate, up-to-date skills. There are two ways the report can be used: one is to focus on the SCANS competencies and foundations, and the other is to focus on jobs. 1992: 529 p.
S/N 029-000-00437-4. $27.00.

Address: Superintendent of Documents
United States Government Printing Office
Washington, DC 20402

Telephone: (202) 783-3238

STANDARD OCCUPATIONAL CLASSIFICATION MANUAL, 1980

Description: Lists occupations and codes, providing a mechanism for cross-referencing and aggregating occupation-related data collected by social and economic statistical reporting programs. Includes a classified list, an alphabetical index, and a listing of the Dictionary of Occupational Titles industries and codes. 1980: 547 p. 1990-repr. Clothbound. S/N 041-001-00351-7. $30.00.

Address: Superintendent of Documents
United States Government Printing Office
Washington, DC 20402

Telephone: (202) 783-3238

SUMMER EMPLOYMENT PROGRAM: THE FEDERAL GOVERNMENT IN PARTNERSHIP WITH EDUCATION

Description: Answers questions for students who would like to work for the Federal Government during the summer months. 1991: Folder. Sold in packages of 50 only. S/N 006-000-01366-0. $10.00.

Address: Superintendent of Documents
United States Government Printing Office
Washington, DC 20402

Telephone: (202) 783-3238

TIPS FOR FINDING THE RIGHT JOB

Description: Includes tips on evaluating your interests and skills, finding job information, writing resumes and application letters, preparing for job interviews, planning your time, and taking tests. 1991: 28 p.; ill. S/N 029-014-00244-5. $1.25.

Address: Superintendent of Documents
United States Government Printing Office
Washington, DC 20402

Telephone: (202) 783-3238

TOMORROW'S JOBS

Description: Identifies the principal factors affecting job prospects and indicates how these factors are expected to affect the occupations in the future. Also includes sections on: Leads to More Information; and Sources of State and Local Job Outlook Information. 1992: 14 p.; ill. S/N 029-001-03093-2. $1.25.

Address: Superintendent of Documents
United States Government Printing Office
Washington, DC 20402

Telephone: (202) 783-3238

TRADE AND EMPLOYMENT

Description: (Quarterly.) A comparison of United States imports in terms of commodity classification based on the Standard Industrial Classification Manual. Subscription price: Domestic - $12.00 a year; Foreign - $15.00 a year. Single copy price: Domestic - $3.25 a copy; Foreign - $4.06 a copy. S/N 703-089-00000-3.

Address: Superintendent of Documents
United States Government Printing Office
Washington, DC 20402

Telephone: (202) 783-3238

UNEMPLOYMENT IN STATES AND LOCAL AREAS

Description: Subscription service includes monthly issues and supplementary material issued irregularly during a 12-month period beginning at time of subscription. Provides provisional, monthly estimates of the labor force, employment, and unemployment for states, metropolitan areas, counties, and cities of 50,000 or more. These estimates are used for economic analysis and administration of various Federal economic assistance programs. Issued in 48X microfiche only. Subscription price: Domestic - $23.00 a year; Foreign - $28.75 a year. S/N 829-002-00000-1.

Address: Superintendent of Documents
United States Government Printing Office
Washington, DC 20402

Telephone: (202) 783-3238

USE OF INTEGRITY TESTS FOR PRE-EMPLOYMENT SCREENING

Description: Examines the available evidence on integrity tests, with emphasis on two basic questions: Has the research on integrity tests produced data that clearly supports or dismisses the assertion that these tests can predict dishonest behavior?; and What public policy issues are raised by the use of integrity tests for pre-employment screening and selection? 1990: 88 p. S/N 052-003-01216-2. $4.00.

Address: Superintendent of Documents
United States Government Printing Office
Washington, DC 20402

Telephone: (202) 783-3238

WHAT WORK REQUIRES OF SCHOOLS, A SCANS REPORT FOR AMERICA 2000

Description: Identifies five competencies and a three-part foundation of skills and personal qualities that lie at the heart of job performance. Also provides three reports on: high-performance work and schools; what is work like today?; and implications for learning. 1991: 62 p.; ill. S/N 029-000-00433-1. $3.25.

Address: Superintendent of Documents
United States Government Printing Office
Washington, DC 20402

Telephone: (202) 783-3238

WHO IS LEAVING THE FEDERAL GOVERNMENT? AN ANALYSIS OF EMPLOYEE TURNOVER

Description: Provides a detailed analysis of the turnover in Federal white-collar occupations. The data on turnover are examined not only by occupations but also from the perspective of major Federal departments, agencies, and selected demographic characteristics of the workforce. 1990: 56 p.; ill. S/N 062-000-00024-4. $3.00.

Address: Superintendent of Documents
United States Government Printing Office
Washington, DC 20402

Telephone: (202) 783-3238

WOMEN AT THIRTYSOMETHING: PARADOXES OF ATTAINMENT

Description: Describes the educational careers and labor market experience of women in the high school class of 1972 through the time they were 32 years old. The paradox of this story, that women's educational achievements were superior to those of men, but that their rewards in the labor market were thin by comparison, is described in the context of national economic development. Written as part of a planned larger study, "Archives of a Generation." 1991: 76 p. S/N 065-000-00451-8. $4.25.

Address: Superintendent of Documents
United States Government Printing Office
Washington, DC 20402

Telephone: (202) 783-3238

WOMEN IN NONTRADITIONAL CAREERS (WINC): JOURNAL AND CURRICULUM GUIDE

Description: The Journal has a plastic spiral binding; the Curriculum Guide is issued in looseleaf form with index dividers. Designed to help educators to increase young women's knowledge of opportunities in the world of work and to help students understand the need for career planning unfettered by traditional options. WINC can be used in high schools, community colleges, youth programs, community-based organizations, and Job Training Partnership Act Programs. The Journal has illustrations and many pages with lines for writing. 1984: 2 bks. (720 p.); ill. S/N 029-002-00074-6. $47.00.

Address: Superintendent of Documents
United States Government Printing Office
Washington, DC 20402

Telephone: (202) 783-3238

WORKER TRAINING: COMPETING IN THE NEW INTERNATIONAL ECONOMY

Description: Focuses on the training given to employed workers both from the standpoint of the competitiveness of United States industry and from the standpoint of the individual worker who may need training to advance. 1990: 288 p.; ill. S/N 052-003-01214-6. $12.00.

Address: Superintendent of Documents
United States Government Printing Office
Washington, DC 20402

Telephone: (202) 783-3238

WORKFORCE 2000: WORK AND WORKERS FOR THE 21ST CENTURY

Description: Predicts trends for the next 15 years and discusses policy issues. Recognizes six challenges: stimulating world growth; improving productivity in the service industries; improving the dynamism of an aging workforce; reconciling the needs of women, work, and families; integrating Blacks and Hispanics fully into the workforce; and improving workers' education and skills. 1987: 145 p.; ill. S/N 029-014-00240-2. $4.25.

Address: Superintendent of Documents
United States Government Printing Office
Washington, DC 20402

Telephone: (202) 783-3238

WORKING WOMAN'S GUIDE TO HER JOB RIGHTS

Description: Provides general information about Federal legislation that affects women's rights when they are seeking a job, while on the job, and when they retire. 1988: 68 p.; ill. S/N 029-002-00072-0. $2.00.

Address: Superintendent of Documents
United States Government Printing Office
Washington, DC 20402

Telephone: (202) 783-3238

Superintendent of Documents Order Form

S044
Please type or print

ORDER BY PHONE: (202) 783-3238
8 a.m. - 4 p.m. eastern time

To fax your orders (202) 512-2250
(24 hours a day, 7 days a week)

Customer's Name and Address

ZIP

Ship To: (If other than address at left)

ZIP

( )
Customer's Daytime Telephone Number

Your order number _____

Date _____

NOTE: Prices include regular domestic postage and handling and are subject to change. International customers please add 25%.

Publications

Qty.	Stock Number	Title	Price Each	Total Price
		Total for Publications		

Subscriptions

Qty.	(List ID)	Title	Price Each	Total Price
		Total for Subscriptions		
		Total Cost of Order		

For privacy protection, check the box below:

☐ Do not make my name available to other mailers

Please choose method of payment:

☐ Check Payable to the Superintendent of Documents

☐ GPO Deposit Account ☐☐☐☐☐☐☐–☐

☐ VISA or MasterCard Account

☐☐☐☐☐☐☐☐☐☐☐☐☐☐☐☐☐☐☐☐

☐☐☐☐ (Credit card expiration date)

_____
(Authorizing Signature)

Thank you for your order!

MAIL ORDER TO:

Superintendent of Documents
P.O. Box 371954
Pittsburgh, PA 15250-7954

CITY PERSONNEL OFFICES

The following section features an alphabetical listing of the names and locations of personnel departments for selected major city and municipal governments found throughout the United States. Recorded jobline telephone numbers are listed where available.

ALAMEDA, CA

Department: Personnel Department

Address: City of Alameda
2263 Santa Clara
Alameda, CA 94501

Telephone: (510) 748-4500   **Jobline: (510) 748-4635**

ALBANY, NY

Department: Personnel Department

Address: City of Albany
City Hall, Room 256M
Albany, NY 12207

Telephone: (518) 434-5049

ALBUQUERQUE, NM

Department: Personnel Department

Address: City of Albuquerque
400 Market St., P.O. Box 1293
Albuquerque, NM 87103

Telephone: (505) 768-3705

ANAHEIM, CA

Department: Personnel Department

Address: City of Anaheim
200 S. Anaheim Blvd.
Anaheim, CA 29805

Telephone: (714) 254-5100   **Jobline: (714) 254-5197**

ANCHORAGE, AK

Department: Employment Department

Address: Municipality of Anchorage
P.O. Box 196650
Anchorage, AK 99519-6650

Telephone: (907) 343-4452   **Jobline: (907) 343-4451**

ATLANTA, GA

Department: Employment Services

Address: City of Atlanta
68 Mitchell Street SW
Atlanta, GA 30035-0306

Telephone: (404) 330-6369   **Jobline: (404) 330-6456**

ATLANTIC CITY, NJ

Department: Personnel Department

Address: City of Atlantic City
City Hall Room 703, 1301 Baccarat Blvd.
Atlantic City, NJ 08401

Telephone: (609) 347-5453

AUSTIN, TX

Department: Personnel Department

Address: City of Austin
2100 E. St., Elmo Building 30E   **Joblines:**
Austin, TX 78744   **(512) 399-3202** Professional
                                (512) 499-3204 Technical
Telephone: (512) 499-2000   **(512) 499-3203** Clerical

BALTIMORE, MD

Department: Personnel Department

Address: City of Baltimore
311 West Saratoga Street
Baltimore, MD 21201

Telephone: (410) 396-3100

BEAVERTON, OR

Department: Personnel Department

Address: City of Beaverton
4755 SW Griffith Dr.
Beaverton, OR 97005

Telephone: (503) 526-2222   **Jobline: (503) 526-2299**

BERKELEY, CA

Department: Personnel Department

Address: City of Berkeley
2180 Milvee Street
Berkeley, CA 94704

Telephone: (510) 644-6460   **Jobline: (510) 644-6122**

BILLINGS, MT

Department: Personnel Department

Address: City of Billings
P.O. Box 1178
Billings, MT 59103

Telephone: (406) 657-8265   **Jobline: (406) 657-8441**

BIRMINGHAM, AL

Department: Jefferson County Personnel Department

Address: City of Birmingham
Room 301A, Courthouse Annex
Birmingham, AL 35263

Telephone: (205) 325-1436

BOCA RATON, FL

Department: Personnel Department

Address: City of Boca Raton
201 Palmetto Park Road
Boca Raton, FL 33432-3795

Telephone: (407) 393-7804   **Jobline: (407) 393-7981**

BOISE, ID

Department: Personnel Department

Address: City of Boise
P.O. Box 500
Boise, ID 83701

Telephone: (208) 384-3850   **Jobline: (208) 384-3855**

BOSTON, MA

Department: Office of Personnel Management

Address: City of Boston
Boston City Hall, Room 612, One City Hall Plaza
Boston, MA 02201

Telephone: (617) 635-3363

BOULDER, CO

Department: Human Resources Department

Address: City of Boulder
P.O. Box 791
Boulder, CO 80306

Telephone: (303) 441-3042   **Jobline:** (303) 441-3434

BUFFALO, NY

Department: Personnel Department

Address: City of Buffalo
65 Niagara Square
Buffalo, NY 14202

Telephone: (716) 851-4200

BURLINGTON, VT

Department: Personnel Department

Address: City of Burlington
City Hall, Church Street
Burlington, VT 05401

Telephone: (802) 658-9300   **Jobline:** (802) 865-7147

CASPER, WY

Department: Human Resource Department

Address: City of Casper
200 N. David
Casper, WY 82601

Telephone: (307) 235-8289

CEDAR RAPIDS, IA

Department: Personnel Department

Address: City of Cedar Rapids
Veterans Memorial Building, First Ave. Bridge
Cedar Rapids, IA 52401

Telephone: (319) 398-5000   **Jobline: (319) 363-7000**

CHANDLER, AZ

Department: Personnel Department

Address: City of Chandler
25 S. Arizona Place, Suite 201
Chandler, AZ 85225

Telephone: (602) 786-2290   **Jobline: (602) 786-2294**

CHARLESTON, SC

Department: City Personnel

Address: City of Charleston
701 E. Bay Street, PCC 1408
Charleston, SC 29403

Telephone: (803) 724-7388   **Jobline: (803) 720-3907**

CHARLESTON, WV

Department: Personnel Department

Address: City of Charleston
P.O. Box 2749
Charleston, WV 25330

Telephone: (304) 348-8015

CHARLOTTE, NC

Department: Human Resources Department

Address: City of Charlotte
600 East Trade St.
Charlotte, NC 28202

Telephone: (704) 336-2287   **Jobline: (704) 336-3968**

CHEYENNE, WY

Department: Personnel Department

Address: City of Cheyenne
2101 O'Neil Ave., Room 103
Cheyenne, WY 82001

Telephone: (307) 637-6341

CHICAGO, IL

Department: Dept. of Personnel

Address: City of Chicago
Room 1100, City Hall, 121 N. LaSalle St.
Chicago, IL 60602

Telephone: (312) 744-4920   **Jobline: (312) 744-1369**

COLORADO SPRINGS, CO

Department: Human Resources Department

Address: City of Colorado Springs
30 S. Nevada Ave.
Colorado Springs, CO 80306

Telephone: (719) 578-6680

COLUMBIA, SC

Department: Employment Division

Address: City of Columbia
P.O. Box 147
Columbia, SC 29217

Telephone: (803) 733-8264   **Jobline: (803) 733-8478**

CONCORD, CA

Department: Personnel Department

Address: City of Concord
1950 Parkside Drive
Concord, CA 94519

Telephone: (510) 671-3308   **Jobline: (510) 671-3151**

CORVALLIS, OR

Department: Personnel Department

Address: City of Corvallis
P.O. Box 1083
Corvallis, OR 97339-1083

Telephone: (503) 757-6902   **Jobline: (503) 757-6955**

DALLAS, TX

Department: Personnel Department

Address: City of Dallas
1500 Marilla, Room 6A North
Dallas, TX 75201

Telephone: (214) 670-3552   **Jobline: (214) 670-5908**

DAVIS, CA

Department: Personnel Department

Address: City of Davis
23 Russell Blvd.
Davis, CA 95616

Telephone: (916) 757-5644   **Jobline: (916) 757-5645**

DAYTONA BEACH, FL

Department: Civil Service Department

Address: City of Daytona Beach
P.O. Box 2451
Daytona Beach, FL 32115-2451

Telephone: (904) 258-3168   **Jobline: (904) 258-3167**

DELRAY BEACH, FL

Department: Human Resources Department

Address: City of Delray Beach
100 NW 1st Ave.
Delray Beach, FL 33444

Telephone: (407) 243-7080   **Jobline: (407) 243-7085**

DENVER, CO

Department:	Personnel Department
Address:	City of Denver 110 16th Street Denver, CO 80202-5206
Telephone:	(303) 640-2151 **Jobline:** (303) 640-1234

DES MOINES, IA

Department:	Personnel Department
Address:	City of Des Moines 400 E. First St. Des Moines, IA 50309
Telephone:	(515) 283-4189 **Jobline:** (515) 283-4115

DETROIT, MI

Department:	Personnel Department
Address:	City of Detroit 2 Woodward Ave., Room 314 Detroit, MI 48226
Telephone:	(313) 224-3700 **Jobline:** (313) 224-6928

DOVER, DE

Department:	Human Resource Department
Address:	City of Dover P.O. Box 475 Dover, DE 19903
Telephone:	(302) 736-7073

EUGENE, OR

Department:	Human Resources Department
Address:	City of Eugene 777 Pearl St., Room 101 Eugene, OR 97401
Telephone:	(503) 687-5061 **Jobline:** (503) 687-5060

EVERETT, WA

Department: Personnel Department

Address: City of Everett
3002 Wetmore
Everett, WA 98201

Telephone: (206) 259-8767   **Jobline:** (206) 259-8768

FAIRBANKS, AK

Department: Personnel Department

Address: City of Fairbanks
14 Cushman
Fairbanks, AK 99701

Telephone: (907) 459-6780

FAIRFIELD, CA

Department: Personnel Department

Address: City of Fairfield
1000 Webster St.
Fairfield, CA 94533

Telephone: (707) 428-7551   **Jobline:** (707) 428-7396

FARGO, ND

Department: Personnel Department

Address: City of Fargo
200 N. Third
Fargo, ND 58102

Telephone: (701) 241-1321

FAYETTEVILLE, AR

Department: Employment Security Department

Address: City of Fayetteville
P.O. Box 1205
Fayetteville, AR 72702

Telephone: (501) 521-5730

FLAGSTAFF, AZ

Department: Personnel Department

Address: City of Flagstaff
211 West Aspen
Flagstaff, AZ 86001

Telephone: (602) 774-5281

FORT COLLINS, CO

Department: Employment Department

Address: City of Fort Collins
P.O. Box 580
Ft. Collins, CO 80522

Telephone: (303) 221-6500   **Jobline: (303) 221-6586**

FORT MEYERS, FL

Department: Human Resources

Address: City of Fort Meyers
P.O. Drawer 2217
Fort Meyers, FL 33902-2217

Telephone: (813) 332-6775   **Jobline: (813) 334-1251**

FORT SMITH, AR

Department: Personnel Department

Address: City of Fort Smith
P.O. Box 1908
Fort Smith, AR 72902

Telephone: (501) 784-2221

FORT WAYNE, IN

Department: Personnel Department

Address: City of Fort Wayne
Room 380, City County Building, One Main Street
Fort Wayne, IN 46802

Telephone: (219) 427-1180   **Jobline: (219) 427-1186**

FRESNO, CA

Department: Personnel Department

Address: City of Fresno
2600 Fresno Street, 1st Floor
Fresno, CA 93721

Telephone: (209) 498-1574   **Jobline: (209) 498-1573**

GLENNDALE, AZ

Department: Personnel Department

Address: City of Glenndale
5850 West Glenndale Ave.
Glenndale, AZ 85301

Telephone: (602) 435-4250   **Jobline: (602) 435-4402**

GRAND JUNCTION, CO

Department: Personnel Department

Address: City of Grand Junction
250 North 5th
Grand Junction, CO 81501

Telephone: (303) 244-1512   **Jobline: (303) 244-1449**

GRAND RAPIDS, MI

Department: Human Resources

Address: City of Grand Rapids
300 Monroe NW, Room 816
Grand Rapids, MI 49503

Telephone: (616) 456-3176

GREEN BAY, WI

Department: Personnel Department

Address: City of Green Bay
100 N. Jefferson, Room 500
Green Bay, WI 54301

Telephone: (414) 448-3147

GREENSBORO, NC

Department: City Employment

Address: City of Greensboro
P.O. Box 3136
Greensboro, NC 27402-3136

Telephone: (919) 373-2088   **Jobline: (919) 373-2080**

GREENVILLE, SC

Department: Personnel Department

Address: City of Greenville
P.O. Box 2207
Greenville, SC 29602

Telephone: (803) 467-4530

HARRISBURG, PA

Department: Bureau of Human Resources

Address: City of Harrisburg
10 N. Market Square, Suite 303
Harrisburg, PA 17101

Telephone: (717) 255-6475

HARTFORD, CT

Department: Personnel Department

Address: City of Hartford
550 Main Street
Hartford, CT 06103

Telephone: (203) 722-6340

HAYWARD, CA

Department: Personnel Department

Address: City of Hayward
25151 Clawiter Rd.
Hayward, CA 94545

Telephone: (510) 293-5000   **Jobline: (510) 293-5313**

HELENA, MT

Department: Personnel Department

Address: City of Helena
316 North Park Ave.
Helena, MT 59623

Telephone: (406) 447-8404

HONOLULU, HI

Department: Personnel Department

Address: City of Honolulu
830 Punchbowl St.
Honolulu, HI 96813

Telephone: (808) 587-0974

HOUSTON, TX

Department: Personnel Department

Address: City of Houston
P.O. Box 1562
Houston, TX 77251

Telephone: (713) 658-3701

HUNTINGTON BEACH, CA

Department: Personnel Department

Address: City of Huntington Beach
2000 Main Street
Huntington Beach, CA 92648

Telephone: (714) 536-5511   **Jobline:** (714) 374-1570

HUNTSVILLE, AL

Department: Department of Human Resources

Address: City of Huntsville
P.O. Box 308
Huntsville, AL 35804

Telephone: (205) 532-7308   **Jobline:** (205) 535-4942

IDAHO FALLS, ID

Department: City of Personnel

Address: City of Idaho Falls
P.O. Box 50220
Idaho Falls, ID 83405

Telephone: (208) 529-1248

INDIANAPOLIS, IN

Department: Human Resources Recruiting

Address: City of Indianapolis, City County Bldg.
200 E. Washington, Suite 1521
Indianapolis, IN 46204

Telephone: (317) 327-5219

IRVINE, CA

Department: Personnel Department

Address: City of Irvine
P.O. Box 19575
Irvine, CA 92713

Telephone: (714) 724-6000   **Jobline: (714) 724-6096**

JACKSON, MS

Department: Personnel Department

Address: City of Jackson
218 S. President
Jackson, MS 39205

Telephone: (601) 960-1053   **Jobline: (601) 960-1003**

JACKSONVILLE, FL

Department: Personnel Department

Address: City of Jacksonville
220 East Bay St., City Hall, Room 107
Jacksonville, FL 32202

Telephone: (904) 630-1111   **Jobline: (904) 630-1144**

JUNEAU, AK

Department: Personnel Department

Address: City of Juneau
                    1555 Seward St.
                    Juneau, AK 99801

Telephone: (907) 586-5278

KANSAS CITY, KS

Department: Personnel Department

Address: City of Kansas City
                    701 N. 7th
                    Kansas City, KS 66101

Telephone: (913) 573-5660   **Jobline: (913) 573-5688**

KNOXVILLE, TN

Department: Civil Service Merit Board

Address: City of Knoxville
                    City/County Building, Suite 1569, 400 Main St.
                    Knoxville, TN 37902

Telephone: (615) 521-2106   **Jobline: (615) 521-2562**

LANSING, MI

Department: Personnel Services Department

Address: City of Lansing
                    1st Floor, City Hall Annex
                    Lansing, MI 48933

Telephone: (517) 483-4004

LAS VEGAS, NV

Department: Personnel Department

Address: City of Las Vegas
                    601 E. Freemont
                    Las Vegas, NV 89101

Telephone: (702) 229-3497   **Jobline: (702) 229-3968 or 3967**

LEXINGTON, KY

Department: Personnel Department

Address: Lexington/Fayette Urban County Government
200 E. Main Street
Lexington, KY 40507

Telephone: (606) 258-3000

LINCOLN, NE

Department: Personnel Department

Address: City of Lincoln
555 S. 10th St., Room B-113
Lincoln, NE 68508

Telephone: (402) 471-7596   **Jobline: (402) 441-7736**

LITTLE ROCK, AR

Department: Personnel Department

Address: City of Little Rock
500 West Marcham, Room 130 West
Little Rock, AR 72201

Telephone: (501) 371-4505

LONG BEACH, CA

Department: Personnel Department

Address: City of Long Beach
333 West Ocean Blvd., 7th Floor
Long Beach, CA 90802

Telephone: (310) 590-6202   **Jobline: (310) 590-6201**

LOS ANGELES, CA

Department: Employment Department

Address: City of Los Angeles
City Hall East, Room 100, 111 E. First St.
Los Angeles, CA 90012

Telephone: (213) 485-2468   **Jobline: (213) 485-2441**

LOUISVILLE, KY

Department:	Recruitment Division
Address:	City of Louisville 609 West Jefferson Louisville, KY 40202
Telephone:	(502) 625-3333 **Jobline: (502) 625-3355**

MADISON, WI

Department:	Department of Human Resources
Address:	City of Madison 210 Martin Luther King Jr. Blvd., Room 501 Madison, WI 53709
Telephone:	(608) 266-4615 **Jobline: (608) 266-6500**

MANCHESTER, NH

Department:	Personnel Department
Address:	City of Manchester 27 Market St. Manchester, NH 03101
Telephone:	(603) 624-6543

MEMPHIS, TN

Department:	Personnel Department
Address:	City of Memphis 125 North Mint American Mall, Room 1B33 Memphis, TN 38103
Telephone:	(901) 576-6509 **Jobline: (901) 576-6548**

MESA, AZ

Department:	Department of Mesa Personnel
Address:	City of Mesa P.O. Box 1466 Mesa, AZ 85211-1466
Telephone:	(602) 644-2365 **Jobline: (602) 644-2759**

MIAMI, FL

Department: Personnel Department

Address: City of Miami
                400 NW Second Ave.
                Miami, FL 33128

Telephone: (305) 579-6111   Jobline: (305) 579-2471

MILWAUKEE, WI

Department: Personnel Department

Address: City of Milwaukee
                200 E. Wells, Room 706
                Milwaukee, WI 53202-3554

Telephone: (414) 286-3751   Jobline: (414) 278-5555

MINNEAPOLIS, MN

Department: Personnel Department

Address: City of Minneapolis
                312 Third Ave. South
                Minneapolis, MN 55415

Telephone: (612) 673-2282   Jobline: (612) 673-2666

MODESTO, CA

Department: Personnel Department

Address: City of Modesta
                P.O. Box 642
                Modesto, CA 95353

Telephone: (209) 577-5200   Jobline: (209) 577-5498

MONTEREY, CA

Department: Personnel Department

Address: City of Monterey
                City Hall
                Monterey, CA 93940

Telephone: (408) 646-3760   Jobline: (408) 646-3751

MONTGOMERY, AL

Department: Department of City/County Personnel

Address: City of Montgomery
P.O. Box 1111
Montgomery, AL 36101-1111

Telephone: (205) 241-4417   **Jobline: (205) 241-2217**

NAPA, CA

Department: Personnel Department

Address: City of Napa
P. O. Box 660
Napa, CA 94559

Telephone: (707) 257-9505   **Jobline: (707) 257-9542**

NASHVILLE, TN

Department: Personnel Department

Address: City of Nashville
214 Stahlman Building, 3rd & Union
Nashville, TN 37201

Telephone: (615) 862-6641   **Jobline: (615) 862-6660**

NEW HAVEN, CT

Department: Personnel/Civil Service Department

Address: City of New Haven
200 Orange Street, Room 404
New Haven, CT 06510

Telephone: (203) 787-8252   **Jobline: (203) 787-8265**

NEW LONDON, CT

Department: Personnel Department

Address: City of New London
181 State Street
New London, CT 06320

Telephone: (203) 447-5210

NEW ORLEANS, LA

Department: Civil Service Department

Address: City of New Orleans
City Hall, 1300 Pardido Street
New Orleans, LA 70112

Telephone: (504) 586-4311

NEW YORK, NY

Department: Employment Department

Address: City of New York
220 Church St.
New York, NY 10013

Telephone: (212) 487-6501

NEWARK, NJ

Department: Personnel Department

Address: City of Newark
920 Broad St.
Newark, NJ 07102

Telephone: (201) 733-8002

NORFOLK, VA

Department: Department of Human Resources

Address: City of Norfolk
100 City Hall Building
Norfolk, VA 23510

Telephone: (804) 441-2239   **Jobline: (804) 627-8768**

OAKLAND, CA

Department: Personnel Department

Address: City of Oakland
505 14th Street, Suite 101
Oakland, CA 94612

Telephone: (510) 238-3526   **Jobline: (510) 238-3111**

OKLAHOMA CITY, OK

Department:	Personnel Department
Address:	City of Oklahoma City 201 Channing Square, B8 Oklahoma City, OK 73102
Telephone:	(405) 297-2530 **Jobline: (405) 297-2419**

OMAHA, NE

Department:	Personnel Department
Address:	City of Omaha Room 506, 1819 Farnam St. Omaha, NE 68183
Telephone:	(402) 444-5302

ORLANDO, FL

Department:	Personnel Department
Address:	City of Orlando 400 S. Orange Ave. Orlando, FL 32801-3302
Telephone:	(407) 246-2121

OXNARD, CA

Department:	Personnel Department
Address:	City of Oxnard 325 S. Eighth St. Oxnard, CA 93030
Telephone:	(805) 385-7590 **Jobline: (805) 385-7580**

PALO ALTO, CA

Department:	Human Resources Department
Address:	City of Palo Alto 250 Hamilton Ave. Palo Alto, CA 94301
Telephone:	(415) 329-2222

PEORIA, IL

Department: Personnel Department

Address: City of Peoria, City Hall Bldg.
419 Fulton Street, Room 203
Peoria, IL 61602

Telephone: (309) 672-8575

PHILADELPHIA, PA

Department: Personnel Department

Address: City of Philadelphia
1600 Arch Street, 15th Floor
Philadelphia, PA 19103-1628

Telephone: (215) 686-2358

PHOENIX, AZ

Department: Phoenix Department of Personnel

Address: City of Phoenix
135 North 2nd Ave.
Phoenix, AZ 85003

Telephone: (602) 262-6608   **Jobline:** (602) 252-5627

PIERRE, SD

Department: Personnel Department

Address: City of Pierre
P.O. Box 1253
Pierre, SD 57501

Telephone: (605) 224-7341

PINE BLUFF, AR

Department: Personnel Department

Address: City of Pine Bluff
200 E. 8th Ave.
Pine Bluff, AR 71601

Telephone: (501) 543-1840

PITTSBURGH, PA

Department: Personnel/Civil Service Commission

Address: City of Pittsburgh
                 City/County Building, 414 Grant Street, Room 401
                 Pittsburgh, PA 15219

Telephone: (412) 255-2710   **Jobline: (412) 255-2388**

PORTLAND, ME

Department: Human Resources

Address: City of Portland
                 389 Congress Street
                 Portland, ME 04101

Telephone: (207) 874-8624

PORTLAND, OR

Department: Personnel Bureau Services

Address: City of Portland
                 City Hall, Room 100, 1220 SW 5th Avenue
                 Portland, OR 97204

Telephone: (503) 823-4352   **Jobline: (503) 823-4573**

PROVIDENCE, RI

Department: Personnel Department

Address: City of Providence
                 25 Dorrance Street
                 Providence, RI 02903

Telephone: (401) 421-7740

PUEBLO, CO

Department: Personnel Department

Address: City of Pueblo
                 P.O. Box 1427
                 Pueblo, CO 81002

Telephone: (719) 584-0815

RALEIGH, NC

Department: Personnel Department

Address: City of Raleigh
P.O. Box 590
Raleigh, NC 27602

Telephone: (919) 890-3315   Jobline: (919) 890-3305

REDMOND, WA

Department: Human Resources Department

Address: City of Redmond
15670 NE 85th St.
Redmond, WA   98052

Telephone: (206) 556-2120   Jobline: (206) 556-2121

RENO, NV

Department: Personnel Department

Address: City of Reno
P.O. Box 1900
Reno, NV 89505

Telephone: (702) 334-2285   Jobline: (702) 334-2287

RICHMOND, VA

Department: Personnel Department

Address: City of Richmond
Room 109 City Hall
Richmond, VA 23219

Telephone: (804) 780-7000   Jobline: (804) 780-5888

SACRAMENTO, CA

Department: Personnel Department

Address: City of Sacramento
813 Sixth St.
Sacramento, CA 95814

Telephone: (916) 264-5726   Jobline: (916) 443-9990

ST. LOUIS, MO

Department:	Personnel Department
Address:	City of St. Louis, Exam Division 1200 Market, Room 100 City Hall St. Louis, MO 63103
Telephone:	(314) 622-4308

ST. PAUL, MN

Department:	Personnel Department
Address:	City of St. Paul 230 City Hall Annex St. Paul, MN 55102
Telephone:	(612) 298-4221

Jobline: (612) 298-4942

ST. PETERSBURG, FL

Department:	Personnel Department
Address:	City of St. Petersburg Room 107, City Hall, Box 2842, 175 5th St. North St. Petersburg, FL 33731
Telephone:	(813) 893-7171

Jobline: (813) 893-7033

SALEM, OR

Department:	Personnel Department
Address:	City of Salem 555 Liberty St. SE, Room 220 Salem, OR 97301
Telephone:	(503) 588-6161

Jobline: (503) 588-6103

SALT LAKE CITY, UT

Department:	Human Resource Department
Address:	City of Salt Lake City 451 S. State, Room 128 Salt Lake City, UT 84111
Telephone:	(801) 535-7647

Jobline: (801) 535-6625

SAN ANTONIO, TX

Department: Recruitment & Support Division

Address: City of San Antonio
P.O. Box 839966
San Antonio, TX 78283-3966

Telephone: (210) 299-8108   **Jobline: (210) 299-7280**

SAN BERNARDINO, CA

Department: Personnel Department

Address: City of San Bernardino
300 N. D Street
San Bernardino, CA 92418

Telephone: (909) 384-5211

SAN DIEGO, CA

Department: Personnel Department

Address: City of San Diego
921 10th Street, Room 101
San Diego, CA 95814

Telephone: (619) 236-5555   **Jobline: (619) 450-6210**

SAN FRANCISCO, CA

Department: Personnel Department

Address: City of San Francisco
400 Van Ness
San Francisco, CA 94102

Telephone: (415) 554-4000   **Jobline: (415) 557-4888**

SAN JOSE, CA

Department: Human Resources

Address: City of San Jose
801 North First Street, Room 207
San Jose, CA 95110

Telephone: (408) 277-4205   **Jobline: (408) 277-5627**

SANTA ANA, CA

Department: Personnel Department

Address: City of Santa Ana
20 Civic Center Plaza
Santa Ana, CA 92702

Telephone: (714) 647-5400   **Jobline: (714) 953-9675**

SANTA CLARA, CA

Department: Personnel Department

Address: City of Santa Clara
1500 Warburton
Santa Clara, CA 95050

Telephone: (408) 984-5122   **Jobline: (408) 984-3150**

SANTA FE, NM

Department: Personnel Department

Address: City of Santa Fe
P.O. Box 909
Santa Fe, NM 87504

Telephone: (505) 984-6500

SANTA MONICA, CA

Department: Personnel Department

Address: City of Santa Monica
1685 Main Street
Santa Monica, CA 90401

Telephone: (310) 458-8246   **Jobline: (310) 458-8697**

SCOTTSDALE, AZ

Department: Human Resources Department

Address: City of Scottsdale
7575 E. Main St.
Scottsdale, AZ 85251

Telephone: (602) 994-2461   **Jobline: (602) 994-2345**

SEATTLE, WA

Department: Personnel Department

Address: City of Seattle
Dexter Horton Bldg., 710 Second Ave., 12 Floor
Seattle, WA 98104-1793

Telephone: (206) 684-7919   **Jobline: (206) 684-7999**

SHREVESPORT, LA

Department: Personnel Department

Address: City of Shrevesport
1237 Murphy St.
Shrevesport, LA 71130

Telephone: (318) 673-5150

SIOUX FALLS, SD

Department: Personnel Department

Address: City of Sioux Falls
224 W. 9th Street
Sioux Falls, SD 57102

Telephone: (605) 339-7062

SITKA, AK

Department: Personnel Department

Address: City of Sitka
304 Lake Street
Sitka, AK 99835

Telephone: (907) 747-3294

SPOKANE, WA

Department: Personnel Department

Address: City of Spokane, City Hall
808 W. Sparkee Falls Blvd.
Spokane, WA 99201-3327

Telephone: (509) 625-6363   **Jobline: (509) 625-6161**

SPRINGFIELD, IL

Department: Department of Personnel

Address: City of Springfield
City Hall Room 215, Municipal Building
Springfield, IL 62701

Telephone: (217) 789-2446   **Jobline: (217) 789-2440**

STAMFORD, CT

Department: Personnel Department

Address: City of Stamford
888 Washington Blvd.
Stamford, CT 06904

Telephone: (203) 977-4070

STOCKTON, CA

Department: Personnel Department

Address: City of Stockton
425 North Eldorado St.
Stockton, CA 95202

Telephone: (209) 944-8233   **Jobline: (209) 944-8523**

SYRACUSE, NY

Department: Personnel Department

Address: City of Syracuse, Room 712
City Hall Commons, 201 E. Washington St.
Syracuse, NY 13202-1476

Telephone: (315) 448-8780

TACOMA, WA

Department: Human Resource Department

Address: City of Tacoma
747 Market Street, Room 1336
Tacoma, WA 98402-3764

Telephone: (206) 591-5400   **Jobline: (206) 591-5795**

TALLAHASSEE, FL

Department: Employee Relations Department

Address: City of Tallahassee
300 S. Adams
Tallahassee, FL 32301

Telephone: (904) 891-8215   **Jobline: (904) 599-8219**

TAMPA, FL

Department: Personnel Department

Address: City of Tampa
306 E. Jackson St.
Tampa, FL 33602

Telephone: (813) 223-8911   **Jobline: (813) 223-8115**

TEMPE, AZ

Department: Human Resource Department

Address: City of Tempe
140 E. Fifth St., Suite 100
Tempe, AZ 85281

Telephone: (602) 350-8276   **Jobline: (602) 350-8217**

TOPEKA, KS

Department: Department of Job Service

Address: City of Topeka
1430 E. S. Topeka Blvd.
Topeka, KS 66612

Telephone: (913) 296-1715   **Jobline: (913) 271-1313**

TORRANCE, CA

Department: Personnel Department

Address: City of Torrance
3031 Torrance Blvd.
Torrance, CA 90503

Telephone: (310) 328-5310   **Jobline: (310) 618-2969**

TRENTON, NJ

Department:	Personnel Department
Address:	City of Trenton City Hall, Dept. of Admin., 319 East State Street Trenton, NJ 08608
Telephone:	(609) 989-3002

TUCSON, AZ

Department:	Human Resources Department
Address:	City of Tucson P.O. Box 27210 Tucson, AZ 85726-7210
Telephone:	(602) 791-4241 **Jobline:** (602) 791-5068

TULSA, OK

Department:	Personnel Department
Address:	City of Tulsa 200 Civic Center, Suite 105 Tulsa, OK 74103
Telephone:	(918) 596-7427 **Jobline:** (918) 596-7444

TUSCALOOSA, AL

Department:	Department of Personnel
Address:	City of Tuscaloosa P.O. Box 2089 Tuscaloosa, AL 35403
Telephone:	(205) 349-2010

VENTURA, CA

Department:	Personnel Department
Address:	City of Ventura P.O. Box 99 Ventura, CA 93002-0099
Telephone:	(805) 654-7853 **Jobline:** (805) 658-4777

WALNUT CREEK, CA

Department: Human Resources

Address: City of Walnut Creek
               P.O. Box 8039
               Walnut Creek, CA 94596

Telephone: (510) 943-5815   Jobline: (510) 943-5817

WEST SACRAMENTO, CA

Department: Personnel Department

Address: City of West Sacramento
               P.O. Box 966
               West Sacramento, CA 95691

Telephone: (916) 373-5800   Jobline: (916) 371-5669

WICHITA, KS

Department: City Hall Personnel

Address: City of Wichita
               455 North Main
               Wichita, KS 67202

Telephone: (316) 268-4531   Jobline: (316) 268-4537

WILMINGTON, DE

Department: Personnel Department

Address: City of Wilmington
               County Building, 800 N. French Street
               Wilmington, DE 19801

Telephone: (302) 571-4280   Jobline: (302) 571-4666

YUBA CITY, CA

Department: Personnel Department

Address: City of Yuba City
               1201 Civic Center Blvd.
               Yuba City, CA 95993

Telephone: (916) 741-4610   Jobline: (916) 741-4766

YUMA, AZ

Department: Employment Department

Address: City of Yuma
180 West First Street
Yuma, AZ 85364

Telephone: (602) 783-1271

FEDERAL JOB INFORMATION CENTERS

The Office of Personnel Management provides job and career information at Federal Job Information Centers located throughout the United States and the District of Columbia.

Many of their locations sponsor recorded job hotline and employment messages that can be accessed directly from your touch-tone telephone. The following section identifies Federal Job Information Centers located throughout the United States.

ALABAMA, HUNTSVILLE
OPM – Federal Employment Information Center
Building 600, Suite 347
3322 Memorial Parkway, South
Huntsville, AL 35801-5311
(205) 544-5803

ALASKA, ANCHORAGE
OPM – Federal Employment Information Center
222 W. 7th Ave., #22
Anchorage, AK 99513-7572
(907) 271-5821

ARIZONA, PHOENIX
OPM – Federal Employment Information Center
Century Plaza Building, Room 1415
3225 N. Central Ave.
Phoenix, AR 85012
(602) 640-5800

ARKANSAS
(see San Antonio, TX)

CALIFORNIA, LOS ANGELES
OPM – Federal Employment Information Center
9650 Flair Drive, Suite 100A
El Monte, CA 91731
(818) 575-6510

CALIFORNIA, SACRAMENTO
OPM – Federal Employment Information Center
1029 J Street, Room 202
Sacramento, CA 95814
(916) 551-1464

CALIFORNIA, SAN DIEGO
OPM – Federal Employment Information Center
Federal Building
Room 4-S-9
880 Front Street
San Diego, CA 92188
(619) 557-6165

CALIFORNIA, SAN FRANCISCO
OPM – Federal Employment Information Center
211 Main St., 2nd Floor, Room 235
P.O. Box 7405
San Francisco, CA 94120
(415) 744-5627

COLORADO, DENVER
OPM – Federal Employment Information Center
12345 W. Alameda Parkway
P.O. Box 25167
Lakewood, CO 80225
(303) 969-7050

CONNECTICUT
(see Massachusetts)

DELAWARE
(see Philadelphia)

DISTRICT OF COLUMBIA: METROPOLITAN AREA
OPM – Federal Employment Information Center
1900 E St., NW
Room 1416
Washington, DC 20415
(202) 606-2700

FLORIDA, ORLANDO
OPM – Federal Employment Information Center
Commodore Building, Suite 125
3444 McCrory Pl.
Orlando, FL 32803-3701
(407) 648-6148

GEORGIA, ATLANTA
OPM – Federal Employment Information Center
Richard B. Russell Federal Building
Room 940A
75 Spring St., SW
Atlanta, GA 30303
(404) 331-4315

HAWAII, HONOLULU (AND OTHER HAWAIIAN ISLANDS AND OVERSEAS)
Office of Personnel Managment
Federal Building, Room 5316
300 Ala Moana Blvd.
Honolulu, HI 96850
(808) 541-2791
(808) 541-2784
(Overseas Jobs)

IDAHO
(see Washington)

ILLINOIS, CHICAGO
OPM – Federal Employment Information Center
175 W. Jackson Blvd., Room 530
Chicago, IL 60604
(312) 353-6192

INDIANA, INDIANAPOLIS
OPM – Federal Employment Information Center
Minton-Capehart Federal Building, Room 368
575 N. Pennsylvania St.
Indianapolis, IN 46204
(317) 226-7161
(For Clark, Dearborn, & Floyd Counties, see Ohio listing)

IOWA
(see Kansas City, MO)
OPM – Federal Employment Information Center
(816) 426-7757
(For Scott County, see Illinois)
(For Pottawatamie County, see Kansas)

KANSAS, WICHITA
OPM – Federal
Employment
Information Center
One-Twenty Building,
Room 101
120 S. Market St.
Wichita, KS 67202
(316) 269-0552
(For Johnson,
Leavenworth, and
Wyandotte Counties,
see Kansas City, MO)

KENTUCKY (see Ohio)
(for Henderson
County, see Indiana)

**LOUISIANA,
NEW ORLEANS**
OPM – Federal
Employment
Information Center
1515 Poydras St.,
Suite 608
New Orleans, LA 70112
(504) 589-2764

**MAINE
(see Massachusetts)**

**MARYLAND,
BALTIMORE**
OPM – Federal
Employment
Information Center
300 West Pratt St.,
Room 101
Baltimore, MD 21201
(410) 962-3822

**MASSACHUSETTS,
BOSTON**
OPM – Federal
Employment
Information Center
Thos. P. O'Neill, Jr.
Federal Building
10 Causeway St.
Boston, MA 02222-
1031
(617) 565-5900

MICHIGAN, DETROIT
OPM – Federal
Employment
Information Center
477 Michigan Ave.,
Room 565
Detroit, MI 48226
(313) 226-6950

**MINNESOTA,
TWIN CITIES**
OPM – Federal
Employment
Information Center
1 Federal Drive,
Room 501
Bishop Henry Whipple
Federal Building,
Ft. Snelling,
Twin Cities, MN 55111
(612) 725-3430

**MISSISSIPPI
(see Alabama)**

**MISSOURI, KANSAS
CITY**
OPM – Federal
Employment
Information Center
Federal Building,
Room 134
601 E. 12st Street
Kansas City, MO 64106
(816) 426-5702

MISSOURI, ST. LOUIS
OPM – Federal
Employment
Information Center
400 Old Post Office
Building
815 Olive St.
St. Louis, MO 63101
(314) 539-2285

**MONTANA
(see Colorado)**
(303) 969-7052

**NEBRASKA
(see Kansas)**

NEVADA (For Clark,
Lincoln, and Nye
Counties, see Los
Angeles; for all other
Nevada Counties not
listed above, see
Sacramento)

**NEW HAMPSHIRE
(see Massachusetts)**

NEW JERSEY (For
Bergen, Essex, Hudson,
Hunterdon, Middlesex,
Morris, Passaic,
Somerset, Sussex,
Union, and Warren
Counties, see New York
City)

NEW JERSEY (For
Atlantic, Burlington,
Camden, Cape May,
Cumberland,
Gloucester, Mercer,
Monmouth, Ocean,
and Salem Counties,
see Philadelphia)

**NEW MEXICO,
ALBUQUERQUE**
OPM – Federal
Employment
Information Center
505 Marquette Ave.,
Suite 910
Albuquerque, NM
87102
(505) 766-2906

**NEW YORK,
NEW YORK CITY**
OPM – Federal
Employment
Information Center
Jacob K. Javits Federal
Building
Second Floor,
Room 120
26 Federal Plaza
New York, NY 10278
(212) 264-0422/0423

**NEW YORK,
SYRACUSE**
OPM – Federal
Employment
Information Center
P.O. Box 7257
100 S. Clinton St.
Syracuse, NY 13260
(315) 423-5660

**NORTH CAROLINA,
RALEIGH**
OPM – Federal
Employment
Information Center
4407 Bland Road,
Suite 202
Raleigh, NC 27609-
6296
(919) 790-2822

**NORTH DAKOTA
(see Minnesota)**

OHIO, DAYTON
OPM – Federal Employment Information Center
Federal Building, Room 506
200 W. 2nd St.
Dayton, OH 45402
(513) 225-2720
(For Van Wert, Auglaize, Hardin, Marion, Crawford, Richland, Ashland, Wayne, Stark, Carroll, Columbiana Counties, and farther north, see Michigan)

OKLAHOMA
(see San Antonio, TX)

OREGON, PORTLAND
OPM – Federal Employment Information Center
Federal Building, Room 376
1220 SW Third Ave.
Portland, OR 97204
(503) 326-3141

PENNSYLVANIA, HARRISBURG
OPM – Federal Employment Information Center
Federal Buidling, Room 168
P.O. Box 761,
Harrisburg, PA 17108
(717) 782-4494

PENNSYLVANIA, PHILADELPHIA
OPM – Federal Employment Information Center
Wm. J. Green, Jr., Federal Building
600 Arch St.,
Philadelphia, PA 19106
(215) 597-7440

PENNSYLVANIA, PITTSBURGH
OPM – Federal Employment Information Center
Federal Building
1000 Liberty Ave.,
Room 119

Pittsburgh, PA 15222
(Walk-in only. For mail or telephone, see Philadelphia listing)

PUERTO RICO, SAN JUAN
OPM – Federal Employment Information Center
U.S. Federal Building, Room 340
150 Carlos Chardon Ave.
Hato Rey, PR 00918-1710
(809) 766-5242

RHODE ISLAND
(see Massachusetts)

SOUTH CAROLINA
(see Raleigh, NC)

SOUTH DAKOTA
(see Minnesota)

TENNESSEE, MEMPHIS
OPM – Federal Employment Information Center
200 Jefferson Ave., Suite 1312
Memphis, TN
(Walk-in only. For mail or telephone, see Alabama listing.)

TEXAS, CORPUS CHRISTI
(see San Antonio)
(512) 884-8113

TEXAS, DALLAS
OPM – Federal Employment Information Center
1100 Commerce St.
Room 6B10
Dallas, TX 75242
(214) 767-8035

TEXAS, HARLINGEN
(see San Antonio)
(512) 412-0722

TEXAS, HOUSTON
(see San Antonio)
(713) 759-0455

TEXAS, SAN ANTONIO
OPM – Federal Employment Information Center
8610 Broadway, Room 305
San Antonio, TX 78217
(512) 229-6611

UTAH (see Colorado)
(303) 969-7053

VERMONT (see Massachusetts)

VIRGIN ISLANDS (see Puerto Rico)
(809) 774-8790

VIRGINIA, NORFOLK
OPM – Federal Employment Information Center
Federal Building, Room 220
200 Granby St.,
Norfolk, VA 23510-1886
(804) 441-3355

WASHINGTON, SEATTLE
OPM – Federal Employment Information Center
Federal Building, Room 110
915 Second Ave.
Seattle, WA 98174
(206) 553-4365

WEST VIRGINIA (see Ohio)
(513) 225-2866

WISCONSIN (For Dane, Grant, Green, Iowa, Lafayette, Rock, Jefferson Walworth, Milwaukee, Waukesha, Racine, and Kanosha Counties, see Illinois listing) (312) 353-6189 (For all other Wisconsin Counties not listed above, see Minnesota listing)
(612) 725-3430

WYOMING (see Colorado)
(303) 969-7052

STATE EMPLOYMENT SERVICE CENTERS

The following section features state listings of various state employment service centers located throughout the United States.

STATE EMPLOYMENT SERVICE CENTERS

ALABAMA
Employment Service,
Dept. of Ind. Rel.
649 Monroe Street
Montgomery, AL 36130
(205) 261-5364

ALASKA
Employment Service
Empl. Sec. Div.
P.O. Box 3-7000
Juneau, AK 99802
(907) 465-2712

ARIZONA
Department of
Economic Security
P.O. Box 6123
Site Code 730A
Phoenix, AZ 85005
(602) 542-4016

ARKANSAS
Employment Security
Division
P.O. Box 2981
Little Rock, AR 72203
(501) 371-1683

CALIFORNIA
Job Service Division
Empl. Dev. Dept.
800 Capitol Mall
Sacramento, CA 95814
(916) 322-7318

COLORADO
Employment Programs
Div. of Empl. & Trng.
251 East 12th Avenue
Denver, CO 80203
(303) 866-6180

CONNECTICUT
Job Service
CT Labor Department
200 Folly Brook Blvd.
Wethersfield, CT 06109
(203) 566-8818

DELAWARE
Employment &
Training Div.
DE Dept. of Labor
P.O. Box 9029
Newark, DE 19711
(302) 368-6911

**DISTRICT OF
COLUMBIA**
Office of Job Service
Dept. of Empl. Services
500 C Street, NW,
Room 317
Washington, DC
20001
(202) 639-1115

FLORIDA
Dept. of Labor
Empl. Sec. 1320
Executive Center Cir.
300 Atkins Building
Tallahassee, FL 32301
(904) 488-7228

GEORGIA
Employment Service
148 International
Blvd., North
Room 400
Atlanta, GA 30303
(404) 656-0380

HAWAII
Employment Service
Division
Dept. of Labor
& Ind. Rel.
1347 Kapiolani Blvd.
Honolulu, Hl 96814
(808) 548-6468

IDAHO
Operations Div.
Emp. Svc.
Dept. of Empl.
317 Main Street
Boise, ID 83735
(208) 334-3977

ILLINOIS
Employment Services
Employment Security
Division
910 S. Michigan Ave.
Chicago, IL 60605
(312) 793-6074

INDIANA
E.S., Employment
Security Div.
10 North Senate Ave.
Indianapolis, IN 46204
(317) 232-7680

IOWA
Job Service Program
Bureau, Department
of Job Service
1000 East Grand Ave.
Des Moines, IA 50319
(515) 281-5134

KANSAS
Div. of Employment
& Training
Dept. of Human
Resources
401 Topeka Avenue
Topeka, KS 66603
(913) 296-5317

KENTUCKY
Dept. for Employment
Services
275 E. Main Street,
2nd Floor
Frankfort, KY 40621
(502) 564-5331

LOUISIANA
Employment Service
Office of Employment
Security
P.O. Box 94094
Baton Rouge, LA
70804-9094
(504) 342-3016

Career Communications, Inc. • P. O. Box 169 • Harleysville, PA 19438 • Telephone (215) 256-3130 • Fax (215) 256-3136

STATE EMPLOYMENT SERVICE CENTERS

MAINE
Job Service Division
Bureau of Employment
Security
P.O. Box 309
Augusta, ME 04330
(207) 289-3431

MARYLAND
MD Dept. of
Employment &
Economics
Development
1100 North Eutaw St.,
Rm. 701
Baltimore, MD 21201
(301) 383-5353

MASSACHUSETTS
Div. of Employment
Security
Charles F. Hurley
Building
Government Center
Boston, MA 02114
(617) 727-6810

MICHIGAN
Bureau of Employment
Service
Employment Security
Commission
7310 Woodward Ave.
Detroit, Ml 48202
(313) 876-5309

MINNESOTA
Job Service & UI
Operations
690 American Center
Bldg.
150 East Kellogg
St. Paul, MN 55101
(612) 296-3627

MISSISSIPPI
Employment Service
Division
Employment Service
Commission
P.O. Box 1699
Jackson, MS 39215
(601) 354-8711

MISSOURI
Employment Service
Division of
Employment Security
P.O. Box 59
Jefferson City, MO
65104
(314) 751-3790

MONTANA
Job Service/
Employment and
Training Division
P.O. Box 1728
Helena, MT 59624
(406) 444-4524

NEBRASKA
Job Service
NE Dept. of Labor
P.O. Box 94600
Lincoln, NE 68509
(402) 475-8451

NEVADA
Employment Service
Employment Security
Department
500 East Third Street
Carson City, NV 89713
(702) 885-4510

NEW HAMPSHIRE
Employment Service
Bureau
Department of
Employment Security
32 South Main Street
Concord, NH 03301
(603) 224-3311

NEW JERSEY
NJ Dept. of Labor
Labor & Industry Bldg.
CN 058
Trenton, NJ 08625
(609) 292-2400

NEW MEXICO
Employment Service
Employment
Security Department
P.O. Box 1928
Albuquerque, NM
87103
(505) 841-8437

NEW YORK
Job Service Division
NY State Department
of Labor, State Campus,
Building 12 G
Albany, NY 12240
(518) 457-2612

NORTH CAROLINA
Employment Security
Commission of North
Carolina
P.O. Box 27625
Raleigh, NC 27611
(919) 733-7522

NORTH DAKOTA
Employment &
Training Division
Job Service North
Dakota
P.O. Box 1537
Bismarck, ND 58502
(701) 224-2842

OHIO
Employment Service
Division
Bureau of Employment
Services
145 S. Front Street,
Rm. 640
Columbus, OH 43215
(614) 466-2421

OKLAHOMA
Employment Service
Employment Security
Commission
Will Rogers Memorial
Ofc. Bldg.
Oklahoma City, OK
73105
(405) 521 3652

STATE EMPLOYMENT SERVICE CENTERS

OREGON
Employment Service
OR Employment
Division
875 Union Street, N.E.
Salem, OR 97311
(503) 378-3212

PENNSYLVANIA
Bureau of Job Service
Labor 7 Industry
Building, Seventh &
Forster Streets
Harrisburg, PA 17121
(717) 787-3354

PUERTO RICO
Employment Service
Division
Bureau of Employment
Security
505 Munoz Rivera Ave.
Hato Rey, PR 00918
(809) 754-5326

RHODE ISLAND
Job Service Division
Dept. of Employment
Security
24 Mason Street
Providence, RI 02903
(401) 277-3722

SOUTH CAROLINA
Employment Service
P O. Box 995
Columbia, SC 29202
(803) 737-2400

SOUTH DAKOTA
SD Dept. of Labor
700 Governors Drive
Pierre, SD 57501
(605) 773-3101

TENNESSEE
Employment Service
Dept. of Employment
Security
503 Cordell Hull Bldg.
Nashville, TN 37219
(615) 741-0922

TEXAS
Employment Service
Texas Employment
Commission
12th & Trinity, 504BT
Austin, TX 78778
(512) 463-2820

UTAH
Employment Services/
Field Oper.
Dept. Employment
Security
174 Social Hall Avenue
Salt Lake City, UT
84147
(801) 533-2201

VERMONT
Employment Service
Dept. of Employment
and Training
P.O. Box 488
Montpelier, VT 05602
(802) 229-0311

VIRGINIA
Employment Service
VA Employment
Commission
P.O. Box 1258
Richmond, VA 23211
(804) 786-7097

VIRGIN ISLANDS
Employment Service
Employment Security
Agency
P.O. Box 1090
Charlotte Amalie, VI
00801
(809) 776-3700

WASHINGTON
Employment Security
Department
212 Maple Park
Olympia, WA 98504
(206) 753-0747

WEST VIRGINIA
Employment Service
Division
Dept. of Employment
Security
112 California Avenue
Charleston, WV 25305
(304) 348-9180

WISCONSIN
Job Service
P.O. Box 7905
Madison, WI 53707
(608) 266-8561

WYOMING
Employment Service
Employment Security
Commission
P.O. Box 2760
Casper, WY 82602
(307) 235-3611

GOVERNMENT BOOKSTORES & DEPOSITORY LIBRARIES

The following section lists the names and locations of government bookstores and depository libraries found throughout the United States.

GOVERNMENT BOOKSTORES

GPO operates bookstores all around the country where you can browse through the shelves and take your books home with you. Naturally, these stores can't stock all of the more than 20,000 titles in inventory, but they do carry the ones you're most likely to be looking for. And they'll be happy to special order any Government book currently offered for sale. All bookstores accept VISA, MasterCard, and Superintendent of Documents deposit account orders.

Bookstores

ALABAMA

O'Neill Building
2021 Third Ave., North
Birmingham, AL 35203
(205) 731-1056
9:00 AM-5:00 PM

CALIFORNIA

ARCO Plaza, C-Level
505 South Flower Street
Los Angeles, CA 90071
(213) 894-5841
8:30 AM-4:30 PM

Room 1023
Federal Building
450 Golden Gate Ave.
San Francisco, CA
94102
(415) 556-0643
8:00 AM-4:00 PM

COLORADO

Room 117, Federal Bldg.
1961 Stout Street
Denver, CO 80294
(303) 844-3964
8:00 AM-4:00 PM

World Savings Building
720 North Main Street
Pueblo, CO 81003
(303) 544-3142
9:00 AM-5:00 PM

DISTRICT OF COLUMBIA

U.S. Government
Printing Office
710 North Capitol St.
Washington, DC 20401
(202) 275-2091
8:00 AM-4:00 PM

Farragut West
1510 H Street NW
Washington, DC 20005
(202) 653-5075
9:00 AM-5:00 PM

FLORIDA

Room 158
Federal Building
400 W. Bay Street
Jacksonville, FL 32202
(904) 791-3801
8:00 AM-4:00 PM

GEORGIA

Room 100, Federal Bldg.
275 Peachtree St., NE
Atlanta, GA 30343
(404) 331-6947
8:00 AM-4:00 PM

ILLINOIS

Room 1365
Federal Building
219 S. Dearborn Street
Chicago, IL 60604
(312) 353-5133
8:00 AM-4:00 PM

MASSACHUSETTS

Room G25
Federal Building
Sudbury Street
Boston, MA 02203
(617) 565-2488
8:00 AM-4:00 PM

MICHIGAN

Suite 160
Federal Building
477 Michigan Avenue
Detroit, MI 48226
(313) 226-7816
8:00 AM-4:00 PM

MISSOURI

120 Bannister Mall
5600 E. Bannister Road
Kansas City, MO 64137
(816) 765-2256
Mon-Sat 10:00 AM-9:30
PM
Sun 12:00 Noon-6:00
PM

GOVERNMENT BOOKSTORES

NEW YORK

Room 110
26 Federal Plaza
New York, NY 10278
(212) 264-3825
8:00 AM-4:00 PM

OHIO

1st Floor, Federal Bldg.
1240 E. 9th Street
Cleveland, OH 44199
(216) 522-4922
9:00 AM-5:00 PM

Room 207
Federal Building
200 N. High Street
Columbus, Ohio 43215
(614) 469-6956
9:00 AM-5:00 PM

PENNSYLVANIA

Robert Morris Building
100 North 17th Street
Philadelphia, PA 19103
(215) 597-0677
8:00 AM-4:00 PM

Room 118, Federal Bldg.
1000 Liberty Avenue
Pittsburgh, PA 15222
(412) 644-2721
8:30 AM-4:30 PM

TEXAS

Room 1C46,
Federal Building
1100 Commerce Street
Dallas, TX 75242
(214) 767-0076
8:00 AM-4:00 PM

9319 Gulf Freeway
Houston, TX 77017
(713) 229-3515
Mon-Sat 10:00 AM-6:00 PM

WASHINGTON

Room 194, Federal Bldg.
915 Second Avenue
Seattle, WA 98174
(206) 442-4270
8:00 AM-4:00 PM

WISCONSIN

Room 190, Federal Bldg.
517 E. Wisconsin Ave.
Milwaukee, WI 53202
(414) 291-1304
8:00 AM-4:00 PM

RETAIL SALES OUTLET

8660 Cherry Lane
Laurel, MD 20707
(301) 953-7974 or
(301) 792-0262
7:45 AM-3:45 PM

*All stores with the
exception of Houston and
Kansas City are open
Mon-Fri (Houston,
Mon-Sat; Kansas City,
7 days a week).*

FEDERAL REGIONAL DEPOSITORY LIBRARY PROGRAM
Send no checks or orders to these libraries.

The Federal Depository Library Program provides Government publications to designated libraries throughout the United States. The Regional Depository Libraries listed below receive and retain at least one copy of nearly every Federal Government publication either in printed or microfilm form for use by the general public. These libraries provide reference services and inter-library loans; however, THEY ARE NOT SALES OUTLETS. You may wish to ask your local library to contact a Regional Depository to help you locate specific publications, or you may contact the Regional Depository yourself.

DEPOSITORIES

AUBURN UNIV. AT MONTGOMERY LIBRARY
Documents Department
Montgomery, AL 36193
(205) 244-3650

UNIV. OF ALABAMA LIBRARY
Documents Dept.,
Box 870266
Tuscaloosa, AL 35487-0266
(205) 348-6046

ARKANSAS STATE LIBRARY
One Capitol Mall
Little Rock, AR 72201
(501) 682-2326

DEPT. OF LIBRARY ARCHIVES and PUBLIC RECORDS
3rd Floor-State Capitol
1700 West Washington
Phoenix, AZ 85007
(602) 542-4121

CALIFORNIA STATE LIBRARY
Govt. Publications Sect.
Sacramento, CA 95814
(916) 324-4863

UNIVERSITY OF COLORADO LIBRARY
Govt. Pub. Library
Boulder, CO 80309-0184
(303) 492-8834

DENVER PUBLIC LIBRARY
Govt. Pub. Department
1357 Broadway
Denver, CO 80203
(303) 640-8817

CONNECTICUT STATE LIBRARY
Government
Documents Unit
231 Capitol Ave.
Hartford, CT 06106
(203) 566-4971

UNIV. OF FLORIDA LIBRARIES
Library West
Documents Dept.
Gainesville, FL 32611
(904) 392-0366

UNIV. OF GEORGIA LIBRARIES
Govt. Documents Dept.
Athens, GA 30602
(404) 542-8949

UNIV. OF HAWAII LIBRARY
Govt. Documents
Collection
2550 The Mall
Honolulu, HI 96822
(808) 956-8230

UNIV. OF IOWA LIBRARIES
Govt. Publication
Department
Washington &
Hamilton Streets
Iowa City, IA 52242
(319) 335-5925

UNIV. OF IDAHO LIBRARY
Documents Section
Moscow, ID 83843
(208) 885-6344

ILLINOIS STATE LIBRARY
Federal Gov. Doc. Dept.
300 South Second St.
Centennial Building
Springfield, IL 62701
(217) 782-4887

DEPOSITORIES

INDIANA STATE LIBRARY
Serials & Documents Section
140 North Senate Ave.
Indianapolis, IN 46204
(317) 232-3686

UNIVERSITY OF KANSAS
Doc. Collect.
Spencer Lib.
Lawrence, KS 66045
(913) 864-4662

UNIV. OF KENTUCKY LIBRARIES
Govt. Documents & Maps
Lexington, KY 40506
(606) 257-3139

LOUISIANA STATE UNIV. LIB.
Govt. Docs. Dept.
Middleton Library
Baton Rouge, LA 70803-3312
(504) 388-2570

LOUISIANA TECH. UNIV. LIB.
Govt. Documents Dept.
Ruston, LA 71272
(318) 257-4962

BOSTON PUBLIC LIBRARY
Government Docs. Dept.
Boston, MA 02117
(617) 536-5400, x 227

UNIVERSITY OF MARYLAND
McKeldin Lib., Doc. Div.
College Park, MD 20742
(301) 405-9165

UNIVERSITY OF MAINE
Raymond H. Fogler Library
Documents Dept.
Orono, ME 04469
(207) 581-1681

DETROIT PUBLIC LIBRARY
5201 Woodward Ave.
Detroit, MI 48202
(313) 833-1025

LIBRARY OF MICHIGAN
717 West Allegan Street
P.O. Box 30007
Lansing, MI 48909
(517) 373-1307

UNIVERSITY OF MINNESOTA
Government Pubs. Div.
409 Wilson Library
309 19th Avenue South
Minneapolis, MN 55455
(612) 624-0241

UNIVERSITY OF MISSOURI AT COLUMBIA LIBRARY
Govt. Documents
Columbia, MO 65201
(314) 882-6733

UNIV. OF MISSISSIPPI LIBRARY
Documents Dept.
Williams Library
University, MS 38677
(601) 232-5857

UNIV. OF MONTANA
Mansfield Library
Documents Division
Missoula, MT 59812
(406) 243-6700

UNIV. OF NORTH CAROLINA at CHAPEL HILL LIBRARY
BA/SS Div. Documents
Davis Library
Chapel Hill, NC 27599
(919) 962-1151

UNIV. OF NORTH DAKOTA
Chester Fritz Library
Documents Dept.
Grand Forks, ND 58202
(701) 777-4630
(in cooperation with)

NORTH DAKOTA STATE UNIV. LIB.
Documents Office
Fargo, ND
(701) 237-8863

UNIVERSITY OF NEBRASKA - LINCOLN
D. L. Love Mem. Library
Lincoln, NE 68588-0410
(402) 472-2562

NEWARK PUBLIC LIBRARY
5 Washington Street
Newark, NJ 07101-0630
(201) 733-7812

UNIVERSITY OF NEW MEXICO
General Library
Government Pub. & Map Dept.
Albuquerque, NM 87131
(505) 277-5441

DEPOSITORIES

NEW MEXICO STATE LIBRARY
325 Don Gaspar Ave.
Santa Fe, NM 87503
(505) 827-3826

UNIVERSITY OF NEVADA-RENO, LIB.
Govt. Pub. Department
Reno, NV 89557
(702) 784-6579

NEW YORK STATE LIBRARY
Documents Section
Cultural Education Ctr.
Albany, NY 12230
(518) 474-3940

STATE LIBRARY OF OHIO
Documents Dept.
65 South Front Street
Columbus, OH 43266
(614) 644-7061

OKLAHOMA DEPT. OF LIBRARIES
Govt. Documents
200 NE 18th Street
Oklahoma City, OK 73105-3298
(405) 521-2502 x 252

OKLAHOMA STATE UNIV. LIB.
Documents Dept.
Stillwater, OK 74078
(405) 744-6313

PORTLAND STATE UNIV. LIB.
Documents Dept.
P.O. Box 1151
Portland, OR 97207
(503) 725-4126

STATE LIBRARY OF PENN.
Govt. Pub. Section
P.O. Box 1601
Harrisburg, PA 17105
(717) 787-3752

CLEMSON UNIVERSITY
Cooper Library
Documents Dept.
Clemson, SC 29634-3001
(803) 656-5174
(in cooperation with)

UNIVERSITY OF SOUTH CAROLINA
Library
Columbia, SC 29208
(803) 777-4841

TEXAS STATE LIBRARY
U.S. Documents Section
Box 12927
Austin, TX 78711
(512) 463-5455

TEXAS TECH UNIV. LIBRARY
Govt. Documents Dept.
Lubbock, TX 79409
(806) 742-2268

UTAH STATE UNIVERSITY
Merrill Library
UMC 30
Logan, UT 84322-3000
(801) 750-1000, x 2683

UNIVERSITY OF VIRGINIA
Alderman Lib., Public Doc.
Charlottesville, VA 22903
(804) 924-3133

WASHINGTON STATE LIBRARY
Documents Section
Olympia, WA 98504
(206) 753-4027

MILWAUKEE PUBLIC LIBRARY
814 W. Wisconsin Ave.
Milwaukee, WI 53233
(414) 278-2167

STATE HIST. SOCIETY LIBRARY
Govt. Pub. Section
816 State Street
Madison, WI 53706
(608) 262-2781
(in cooperation with)

UNIVERSITY OF WISCONSIN-MADISON
Madison, WI
(608) 262-9852

WEST VIRGINIA UNIV. LIB.
Documents Dept.
Morgantown, WV 26506-6069
(304) 293-3640

The following section features definitions of commonly used labor market information terms.

• AFFIRMATIVE ACTION

A program that became law with the passage of the Equal Opportunity Act of 1972. The law requires employers, labor unions, employment agencies, and labor-management apprenticeship programs to make an affirmative effort to eliminate discrimination against and increase employment of females and minorities. Affirmative action refers to the detailed written plans drawn up by employers for equalizing economic opportunity with respect to hiring, promotion, transfers, wages and salaries, training programs, fringe benefits, and other conditions of employment.

• AGRIBUSINESS

The sector of the economy concerned with the production, processing, and distribution of agricultural products and farm supplies. It also includes businesses that provide agricultural services and economic agencies and financial institutions that serve agricultural producers.

• AREA SAMPLE

A method used to gather statistics on a geographic basis.

• BASE PERIOD

A selected period of time, frequently one year (called a base year), against which changes in other years are calculated. The relationship is usually expressed as base year = 100.

• BENCHMARK STATISTICS

Comprehensive data which are used as a basis for developing and adjusting interim estimates made from sample information.

• BUSINESS CYCLE

A pattern of fluctuation in economic activity, characterized by alternate expansion and contraction. Economists distinguish four phases: (1) expansion; (2) contraction; (3) depression or recession; and (4) recovery.

• CURRENT POPULATION SURVEY (CPS)

A national household survey conducted monthly by the Bureau of the Census for the Bureau of Labor Statistics. The CPS provides a variety of demographic, economic, and social characteristics on the civilian noninstitutional population age 16 and over.

• CYCLICAL INDUSTRY

An industry whose sales and profits reflect the ups and downs of the business cycle. Almost all capital goods industries (steel, machine tools, etc.) are cyclical because any decline in consumer demand may eliminate the demand for the capital goods needed to make the product.

• CYCLICAL UNEMPLOYMENT

Unemployment that is caused by periodic declines in business activity that give rise to an inadequate demand for workers.

• DURABLE GOODS

Items with a normal life expectancy of three years or more. Automobiles and furniture are examples. Durable goods are the most volatile component of consumer expenditures.

• ECONOMETRIC MODEL

A set of related equations used to analyze economic data through mathematical and statistical techniques. Econometric models are used for forecasting, estimating the likely quantitative impact of alternative assumptions, including those of government policies, and for testing various theories about the way the economy works.

• ECONOMIC INDICATOR

A statistical series that has been found to represent fairly accurately the changes in business conditions. The Department of Commerce publishes various economic indicators on a monthly basis in *Business Conditions Digest.*

• ECONOMIC TIME SERIES

A set of quantitative data collected over regular intervals which measures some aspect of economic activity.

• ESTABLISHMENT

An economic unit, such as a farm, mine, factory or store, which produces goods or provides services. It is usually at a single location and engaged in one predominant type of economic activity for which a Standard Industrial Classification (SIC) code is applicable.

• FRICTIONAL UNEMPLOYMENT

The temporary joblessness which results from individuals who are between jobs, are engaged in seasonal work, have quit their jobs and are looking for better ones, or are looking for their first jobs. This type of unemployment is usually short term and is caused by the economy's inability to match jobseekers with jobs immediately.

• FULL EMPLOYMENT

A state of the economy in which all persons who want to work can find employment without much difficulty at the prevailing rates of pay. This does not mean the same thing as zero unemployment because seasonal and frictional unemployment will still exist to some extent.

• FULL-TIME EMPLOYMENT

Generally includes persons who worked 35 hours or more during the survey week (week of the month that includes the 12th). Persons who worked between 1 and 34 hours are designated as working part-time.

• HIGH TECHNOLOGY

A term to indicate the presence of one or more of the following factors: (l) high use of scientific and technical workers, (2) high expenditures for research and development (R&D) activities, (3) the industry's product either uses advanced technologies for its production or is itself an example of advanced technology.

• INDEX NUMBER

A measure of the relative changes occurring in a series of values compared with a base period. The base period usually equals 100, and any changes from it represents percentages.

• INDUSTRY-OCCUPATION (1-0) MATRIX

A tabulation of employment data cross-classified by industry and occupation, arranged in a grid divided into rows and columns. It provides a model representing the occupational employment staffing pattern of each industry for one point in time.

• INITIAL CLAIM

This is a notice filed by a worker at the beginning of a period of unemployment requesting a determination of insured status for jobless benefits.

• MEAN

The simplest of all statistical averages is obtained by adding all the observed values together and dividing by their total number.

• MEDIAN

It is the middle value (or midpoint between two values) in a set of data arranged in order of increasing or decreasing magnitude. As such, one-half of the items in the set are less than the median and one-half are greater.

 Career Communications, Inc. • P. O. Box 169 • Harleysville, PA 19438 • Telephone (215) 256-3130 • Fax (215) 256-3136

• MODE

The most frequently occurring value in a group of values. Like the median, the mode is not influenced by extreme values in the group, but is used less often in statistical analysis than either the median or the mean.

• NONDURABLE GOODS

Items that generally last for only a short time (three years or less). Food, beverages and apparel are examples. Because of the nature of nondurable goods, they are generally purchased when needed.

• REGRESSION ANALYSIS

Widely used in statistics and econometrics as a method for predicting the value a dependent variable from known values of independent variables. For example, it might be used to predict the output of certain production workers (dependent variable) based on the results of testing them for mechanical aptitude (independent variable). Simple regression analysis involves just one independent variable; multiple regression analysis involves several independent variables.

• SAMPLING ERROR

An error arising from the fact that the sample used does not correspond closely enough to the population which it is intended to represent.

• SEASONAL ADJUSTMENTS

Statistical modifications made to data to compensate for predictable fluctuations which recur more or less regularly every year in a time series such as employment rates. Compensations are made for the fluctuations to facilitate the evaluation of the important underlying reasons for the month-to-month changes.

• SEASONAL INDUSTRY

An industry in which business activity is affected by regularly recurring events such as weather changes, holidays, vacations, etc.

• SELF-EMPLOYED WORKER

Describes an individual who works more or less regularly, but usually does so in his/her own home or office. This person is not listed on any establishment's payroll.

- ## STANDARD INDUSTRIAL CLASSIFICATION (SIC) MANUAL

   A reference work published by the Office of Management and Budget that is used to classify establishments on the basis of their primary economic activity. The SIC is structured in a manner that allows establishments to be grouped into both broad and narrow categories.

- ## STRUCTURAL UNEMPLOYMENT

   Long-term joblessness resulting from changes in job skill requirements, job skill obsolescence, and the availability of job skill training programs.

ORDER FORM

HOW TO ORDER:

By Telephone or Fax: For the fastest service, place your order today by telephone (215) 256-3130 or fax (215) 256-3136.

By Mail: Complete this order form and mail with payment to Career Communications, Inc., 298 Main Street, P.O. Box 169, Harleysville, PA 19438.

OUR GUARANTEE

We at Career Communications take pride in the quality of our publications. If you are not completely satisfied with any of our publications, you may return them to us in their original condition within 30 days for a full refund.

Publication	Price	Quantity	Total
American Directory of Job and Labor Market Information	$29.95		
Job Hotlines USA; The National Directory of Employer Joblines	$24.95		

Federal ID Number: 23-2420796

Subtotal	$
Pennsylvania buyers add 6% sales tax.	$
Shipping & Handling Add $4.50 for the first book and $1.50 for each additional book.	$
Total	$

IMPORTANT! This order form is for Career Communications publications only.

METHOD OF PAYMENT:

☐ **Check/money order.** Please find enclosed check payable to Career Communications, Inc. (U.S. dollars only) in the amount of $ _____ .

Credit Card (check one):

☐ VISA   ☐ MasterCard

Card No. _____

Expiration Date _____

Signature _____

☐ **Bill me.** P.O. # _____

SHIP TO:

Please print:

Name _____

Title/Dept. _____

Organization _____

Address _____ Suite _____

City/State _____

Zip Code _____ Telephone (____) _____

Type of Business _____

CAREER COMMUNICATIONS, INC.
298 Main Street, P.O. Box 169, Harleysville, PA 19438
(215) 256-3130